'*The Bible of eBook Publishing.*' MCWRITER, USA

'*Undeniably useful for anyone embarking on the great adventure that is e-publishing. It certainly was for me!*' LOUISE VOSS, UK – Bestselling Kindle Author/100,000+ ebooks sold

'*This is an excellent do-it-yourself book on how to write for e-books. Follow the instructions and you will succeed, It gives you the incentive to write.*' DAVID WARREN, US university professor

'*Very well written and easy to follow, even for a 66 year old like me! I have already published an e book but this showed me how it could have been easier. Should have read this first!*' UK Amazon reader

'*So good. I'm a mainstream published author and just spent the last year researching the ever-changing world of e-books. Stephanie's book was easily the best. So simple. So straightforward.*' JESSICA ADAMS, AUSTRALIA

'*Good Grief... This book has absolutely EVERYTHING in it that anyone thinking about publishing would need or want to know. It is ALL right here.. and I mean every single bit of it... amazing book.*' K GARDNER, US

'*Fantastic. I'm 83 years old, technically naïve as far as computers are concerned. I strongly advise anyone wanting to 'Kindle' their writings to buy Stephanie's book. I did and it saved my sanity.*' ALAN GRAINGER, UK

'*Great, great book. I can't understand how I could ever have managed my way through the ebook process without it. Given the other costs of publishing, the price is just ridiculously low.*' Apple iBooks reviewer

SELF-PUBLISHING EBOOKS

The Absolute Beginner's Step-by-Step Guide

Stephanie Zia
with Mark Binner

blackbird

SELF-PUBLISHING EBOOKS

The Absolute Beginner's Step-by-Step Guide

Stephanie Zia
with Mark Binner

blackbird

Edition 26 – Updated November 2015

This edition published in 2015 by
Blackbird Digital Books 2/25 Earls Terrace London W8 6LP

www.blackbird-books.com

ISBN 9780993092268

A CIP catalogue record for this book is available from the British Library

Cover image ID 9159913 © Juliengrondin | Dreamstime.com

CONTENTS

CHAPTER 1

COPY EDITING – WHY THE END IS ONLY THE BEGINNING

'Add freshly ground black people.' Cookery book misprint, 2010

So, you've written The End and your manuscript is perfect and ready to publish.

Are you sure about that?

Before publication, all print books go through two vital stages: copy editing and proofreading. If it's to look professional, your ebook must do the same. But first, have a close look at your writing one last time.

• Are there any long, rambling sentences that could be shortened or split into two? Large, intense sentences and big blocks of paragraph aren't so easy on the eye scanning a page. With an electronic screen this is even more relevant and especially important for ebooks. In any medium, short sentences and simple words are more likely to keep your reader engaged. Look for 'ands' and 'buts' which could be replaced by full stops.

• Look at the length of your paragraphs. Have you missed any natural breaks that could be split?

• Can you break up the page by taking a list that may appear in a sentence and turn it into a linear list that scans down the page, with one subject on top of the next one, rather than running along horizontally?

• Are there any lists like this one that would benefit from bullet points?

To give you the professional perspective on copy editing and proofreading, I'm handing over to Blackbird Digital Books' Associate Editor Sarah Tomley. Sarah has worked as a copy editor and commissioning editor for some of the UK's largest publishing companies and has edited hundreds of books.

The Difference Between Copy Editing and Proofreading

'Copy editing comes at an earlier stage than proofreading. When you've finished writing, a copy editor will read your book and make sure that it will work from a reader's point of view. Often authors are so expert in their subject that they assume too much knowledge on the part of the reader, and skip into discussions on new subjects without introducing them clearly.

The copy editor's first task is to check the structure of the whole book:

Is it logical?

Is it the best way to guide a reader through a new subject? Does it include everything that the reader needs to know? Does it need an introduction, or explanatory section at the beginning? Non-fiction books, especially 'how to' books, often benefit from having a separate 'key skills' area before the main chunk of the book, which readers can refer back to easily at any time.

Does the book need a glossary?

Or index?

The second thing a copy editor does is to focus in on each section or chapter one at a time. This involves the same kind of structure checking as above, but now focuses only on one section, to make sure its structure make sense, is easy to follow, and includes everything necessary.

Then comes the detailed read, correcting grammar and spelling mistakes, checking that facts, names, dates, references and so on are correct. During this 'pass' over the text, the copy editor will also smooth out the tone and rhythm of the text, in line with the publisher's style. If you're self-publishing a printed book or an ebook, you'll need to decide – as the publisher – what this style is. Some publishers opt for a very detached, authoritative style; others for an expert but friendly approach; a few for an irreverent, cheeky one; and so on.

How closely do you want to speak to your readers? The two things to consider here are what image you want to project (are you a detached expert or the reader's friend?) and who your audience is (do they want detailed information, a humorous rough guide, or just to read your story?).

The copy editor also keeps an eye out for consistency, and works with a running 'list' of spellings, capitalisations, etc. that could be used in more than one way (he or she makes a decision early on and ensures that it is the form used in every instance). Are you opting for 'z' or 's' spellings? (ie specialization or specialisation?) Do you refer to the Earth or the earth? Is there always a space between amounts and units or not? (10 g or 10g?) However something appears in its first use in the book must be used throughout.

In general publishing, digital manuscripts undergo many layers of checks, from the initial read-through and possibly requested rewrite of the submitted manuscript, to three or four editing and proofing checks by the copy editor and designer, and at least two by the author. And even then mistakes can sneak through.

Have someone else check your text for you, to act as the copy editor. You will have seen the text so many times that your brain will skip along too fast, filling in the gaps if there are any – so you'll be blind to them. If you don't have anyone to act as copy editor for you, make sure you leave long enough between writing and editing to be able to approach the text as though seeing it almost for the first time; Stephen King recommends locking away the manuscript for at least six weeks.

Copy Editing Non-Fiction

Does the structure make sense? Check the overall book and the structure of each chapter.

Have you included everything you need/meant to? Are your chapter titles clear and useful? Do you need any repeating devices to help make important points? (These could be as simple as occasional 'top tips' or pictures to illustrate the main points.)

Are your sources 100% reliable?

Have you libelled anybody? (See Chapter 4, Libel)

Are all real towns, districts etc in the place the author says they are and spelled correctly?

Is the tense consistent throughout? (ie do you start off talking in the present tense and veer off to the past or future?)

Is the viewpoint consistent throughout? Are you in the first person, 'I did this, I did that etc' , the second person 'You do this, then you do that etc' or the third person 'He did this, she did that etc' ?

Who is the target audience? Is the book solely for US consumption? Or solely for UK consumption? Like most ebooks, is it going to be sold to a world market simultaneously? If so, are there any regional technicalities that need expanding on or deleting – pricing, contact details, regional phone numbers etc.

Are there sectors that need clarifying for the world audience? Can you insert an American, European or Asian equivalent to any society or organisation that you quote? Whichever route you decide on, local or international, be consistent.

Grammar. Don't rely on computer grammar programs.

Spelling. Don't rely on computer spellcheckers. If you're not sure about a spelling, use an online dictionary.

Fiction

As the novel is its own world within itself, not much of the above is relevant. One important point to check in fiction is timeline.

Are dates and seasons consistent? Does everybody age at the same rate? Are there any minor characters, animals even, that appear and disappear without trace? Are there any quotes that need clearing and paying for or deleting (see Chapter 2: Copyright)? Don't even let the thought cross your mind that it's only your small book and nobody important will ever read it and notice anyway.

Have you made up any fictional names for companies or places that really exist and therefore might, within the context of the story, get you into trouble? Have you mentioned real companies or people who get involved in your fictional story in a less than glowing way which could get you into trouble?

Getting the professionals in

What a professional can give you is a fresh eye. An insight into the actual content of your words – ie what they really say, not what you think they say. Editors know that there are many ways in which communication can fail, but here's three that you're unlikely to spot in your own writing:

Authors often 'delete' (don't say as much as they think they have); 'generalise' (make sweeping statements that aren't strictly true and need unpicking and rephrasing if useful); and 'distort' (introduce a personal bias where it is not appropriate). A professional will very quickly iron out any of these contaminating factors.

Every client has different needs – and only they know the real purpose of the book (to share information, to make money, to shock, and so on). A professional editor will ensure that the book you've written does the job you want.

The depth of a copy edit is up to you to make clear when you commission. Do you want a heavy edit (the full check as given above), or a light proofread (for grammatical/spelling/typographical errors only)? Some authors, for example, would like their copy editor to check their sentence structures and edit the words to flow with a better rhythm and pace. This will give the work that all-important professional sheen. But to many authors this would be nothing short of anathema – a crossing of the line from checking to interfering with their precious words.'

So: make sure you spell out your requirements very clearly before you commission an editor.'

How much will it cost?

Copy editing is much more time-consuming than proofreading – it probably works out at around three to four times the cost. But Sarah points out it's really impossible for a professional to judge without seeing a sample piece, as some people's work needs only a very light edit, while others needs a virtual re-write:

'If you're writing a non-fiction book, think about hiring a professional to help structure it – ie lay out the plan for the whole book and for each chapter – so that the structure makes sense and the writing is easy. By breaking down the chapter – into the content for each chapter and even each page, if you want – it becomes much easier for the author. You can then write in prescribed 'chunks' , and don't have to waste time wondering what to write each day. Once you know that you've included everything that's important, you can just enjoy writing. This is the kind of help you'd expect from the full 'commissioned' service – the full attention and expertise of a professional commissioning editor for one, two or all of the services – detailed structure/planning; copy-editing; and proofreading. Just as any professional author would enjoy when working with a large publishing company.'

Sarah is the MD of the UK company EditorsOnline, a group of top freelance UK editors who work at highly competitive rates. No job is too small or too large, and they're friendly too. For more information go to http://editorsonline.org/.

To get a competitive quote in the USA, search for copy editors/proofreaders at https://www.elance.com/.

Proofreading

Copy editing all done, now it's time for your first proofread. The final one comes at the end of the process, just before you go to print. See Chapter 20 for a checklist.

Top Tip

Cut and paste your document into Google Docs before converting. Go to Tools > Spelling and a window will pop up with change/ignore options. Now you can check through the whole document by clicking Ignore (or choose to Change) each time. Not all suggestions are written-in-stone correct, quite often they are suggested alternatives. There's also an Amazon check system that kicks in just before you publish on Kindle. So when you have your final draft, it's worth converting that to .mobi for Kindle sooner rather than later. Then open up your publication page and load to Amazon KDP's dashboard (you'll be shown how to do all of this in detail later). You don't have to go all the way and publish at this stage. The spellcheck only appears after you have opened the book's file once from Amazon's dashboard. So, open the file, then close it again and you'll see Amazon's helpful list of spelling errors, which they will email to you if you wish.

CHAPTER 2

COPYRIGHT AND COPYLEFT

Copyright extends to 70 years after the author's death in the UK. In the USA it could be 70, 95 or even 120 years.

Wherever you are, even if you've written a work of fiction, you must do a thorough copyright check.

Have you quoted from any books, poems or song lyrics? Have your characters read any magazine or newspaper reports quoted from real life that could get you into trouble (see C3, Libel)?

Music
Have you used any song lyrics? Song lyrics are the bane of professional authors and permissions are often notoriously expensive.

Author Blake Morrison had to pay: £500/$728 for one line of *Jumping Jack Flash*.

£735/$1069 for one line of *When I'm Sixty-four* (I'm quivering a bit here but it IS all right to name the title of the song, even if it's included in a later lyric).

Two lines of *I Shot the Sheriff*?: £1,000/$1455.

His final bill was £4,401.75/$6,406. And that was addressed to the author, not the publisher. He was lucky to have a decent publisher who helped him out by paying half.

Music copyright is complicated. To read more and to find out how to get a quote, go to The UK Copyright Service
https://copyrightservice.co.uk/

or ASCAP (The American Society of Composers, Authors and Publishers)
http://www.ascap.com/.

Words

Whilst every case must be checked individually, generally speaking the 70 years after the author's death in the UK and the pre-1923 Public Domain rule in the US are your starting points. Be aware that works might have been re-licensed. In the process of trying to clear a quotation from a World War 1 memoir we wanted to use in Blackbird Digital Books' French travel book *The Valley of Heaven and Hell, Cycling in the Shadow of Marie Antoinette* by Susie Kelly, the author finally got the definitive response from a US librarian. Whilst the text was all over the web, the copyright was very questionable. There had been numerous other editions, with new introductions, *plus* an original ghostwriter who had died much later than the author! JUST BECAUSE IT'S ON THE INTERNET DOESN'T MEAN IT'S COPYRIGHT FREE! NO WAY!

Images

If you're using photos you took yourself you might think you're clear. But no.

It's a bit of a grey area but if there are any people in your images who are not being photographed in a public place, you are technically supposed to get model clearance if you're putting your picture in a selling document. If you look on photo agency sites the images will say 'model cleared' to show they have signed permission from the person in the photo. If you're in a situation where you can get a chit of paper signed, get it signed.

Many historical or special sites, houses, gardens etc open to the public allow photography. But only for non-commercial use. If you decide to use one of your snaps in your book you'll have to get clearance and permission. We tried to clear a picture of Marie Antoinette's bed in the Palace of Versailles for *The Valley of*

Heaven and Hell. Permission to use one photo for an ebook would have cost 119 Euros ($164/£103).

Whilst old paintings might be out of copyright, the IMAGE of the painting may well not be. Museums and art galleries, many of whom ban photography, grant licenses to use reproductions of their images, for which you have to pay. Some images ARE OK, the Mona Lisa, for example, is obviously everywhere. If the image is pre-1885 you're more likely to be in luck but always check no matter what the date. Most copyright notices are on Wikipedia. But be careful. The rules vary according to where you are. In 2009 the National Portrait Gallery in London threatened to sue an American who uploaded some of their images to Wikipedia. Whilst the images were in the public domain, the digital photos were not – in the UK anyway. A classically complicated case. The museum may require a credit even if there's no payment.

Links

Check the source of your links. In *The Valley of Heaven and Hell* the author had included a fantastic clip from an old Jacques Tati film. It had to come out.

From Wikipedia contributor guidelines: *For policy or technical reasons, editors are restricted from linking to the following, without exception: Material that violates the copyrights of others per contributors' rights and obligations should not be linked. Linking to websites that display copyrighted works is acceptable as long as the website has licensed the work.* ***Knowingly directing others to material that violates copyright may be considered contributory copyright infringement****. If you know that an external website is carrying a work in violation of the work's copyright, do not link to that copy of the work. Linking to a page that illegally distributes someone else's work sheds a bad light on Wikipedia and its editors.* ***This is particularly relevant when linking to sites such as YouTube, where due care should be taken to avoid linking to material that violates copyright.***

Not everything is copyright

Just to complicate matters, there's an area of copyright law called Fair Dealing, or Fair Use, where you can use quotes as long as you document the source. I sometimes quote from websites and books without asking for permission. The rules used to state that you were OK if the quote was used as a small part of a journalistic article and the source given.

Blake Morrison explains that in the UK the guidelines are as follows: 'If you're writing a critical commentary on a piece of writing you can quote up to 400 words or use a series of extracts of up to 800 words. With poetry it's up to 40 lines, provided that doesn't exceed a quarter of the poem's length.' Since the new UK copyright laws of 2014 came into force, it's now OK to use quotes without permission in non-factual pieces as well.

The laws vary from country to country. For more information look at the Fair Dealing section on Wikipedia's Copyright page. Wikipedia itself is copyright free. Its text is available under the Creative Commons Attribution-ShareAlike Licence but additional terms may apply.

There's been plenty of discussion about the accuracy of Wikipedia over the years. I've found it pretty reliable but I prefer to use http://www.encyclopedia.com/ as a first reference point. It searches over 100 encyclopedias and dictionaries and the results can be viewed side-by-side. Whatever your source, facts should always be double-checked, preferably triple-checked via the most reliable sources you can find. Though newspapers have a political bias, their articles will have gone through their own checking procedures. Treat personal blogs with caution, especially if they have an agenda, clear or hidden. Blogs can of course be excellent sources of information you could find in no other way. To check up on the weight and authority of a blog or website, type its name in the Technorati search window. The higher the number the better. The famous internet newspaper The Huffington Post, for example, has an authority of 958. Technorati is also a useful place to go to when you get to your ebook promotion stage (see chapter 26).

If you want to use somebody else's work, an expert in a particular field for example, don't be afraid to seek permission. People are often delighted to be asked. Tell them they'll receive full credit for their quote and don't forget to do that. Thank them in your Acknowledgements and send them a copy of the ebook. Print and file any permission emails in a safe folder so that you can prove it later if need be.

Wherever copyright is concerned, don't ever think, 'ah they're too famous to bother with my little book, I'll probably get away with it'. DON'T RISK IT. Always veer on the side of caution.

Finding Copyright-free Material

Creative Commons is now included in the Firefox Main Search Browser window at the top right of the Web Page, where Google is. Click the little arrow next to the window and go to Creative Commons.

This brings up a very useful search page where you can specify a CC search in Europeana, Google Images, Wikimedia Commons, YouTube, Jamendo (music), Flickr, Fotopedia, Open Clip Art Library, Google Web, SpinXpress Media Note that CC has no control over the results that are returned. *Do not assume that the results displayed in this search portal are under a CC license*. You should always verify that the work is actually under a CC license by following the link. Since there is no registration to use a CC license, CC has no way to determine what has and hasn't been placed under the terms of a CC license. If you are in doubt you should contact the copyright holder directly, or try to contact the site where you found the content.

Photographs and artwork

Have you used any photographs or artwork? Are they copyright-free? Is there a photographer you have to pay? What about the person in the photograph? Have you asked their permission and got a signed clearance?

For licensing permission to use copyrighted artwork, go to http://www.dacs.org.uk/. They represent many of the most famous artists who are still in copyright.

If the work is by a friend or relative, have you asked permission and credited them in your Acknowledgements? For free stock photos go to http://compfight.com/ For free graphics go to http://www.freevector.com/.

There you will find a huge selection of images. Some are free for private use only, others for private and commercial use. There is a special page for commercial use: http://qvectors.net/tag/commercial-use/page/2/.

ALWAYS credit and link, if possible, to the source.

Copyleft

Copyleft is an internet word. It's a form of licensing that's used to maintain copyright on computer software, documents, music and art. It's a novel way of using existing copyright laws to ensure a work remains freely available. See Wikipedia for more information.

Your Own Copyright

Copyright Notices

Put a copyright notice at the front of your book, the symbol © plus the word 'copyright' plus any disclaimers. If you're offering advice make it clear you're not legally responsible for anybody else's actions.

The copyright sign on a Mac is ALT + G. The copyright sign on a PC is CTRL + Alt + C *or* Alt + 0169 (on block of no's far R of keyboard). Or in Word: INSERT> symbol.

CHAPTER 3

WHY THERE'S NO NEED TO GET CONFUSED BY ALL THE DIFFERENT EBOOK FORMATS

The Basics

Basically one main master Word document will, with slight adaptations, cover the four ebook formatting systems. Before we go any further, you may want to create your ebooks for Amazon Kindle (and perhaps PDF format for paperback) ONLY. Their formatting system is called Mobi.

I did this for a while because I chose to enrol my ebooks into Amazon's KDP Select where exclusivity is a requirement. You are only locked in for 3 months at a time and can leave at any juncture. This doesn't suit everybody (see the debates online) but, for me the discoverability opportunities Amazon's promotional arm offers outweighed the wider reach.

To save you wasting any time, I recommend you examine the pros and cons of joining Amazon KDP Select before deciding which format(s) you are going to make your ebook in. The advantages and disadvantages change all the time as Amazon move the goalposts backwards and forwards!

In Dec 2014 there was a big swing away from Amazon exclusivity, due to a marked loss of revenue for many independent authors. This came about after the introduction of Amazon's subscription service Kindle Unlimited (KU): a kind of free library system for readers, and compulsory for your books if you enrol them in KDP Select. (Why would you in the first place? For higher visibility on Amazon's pages via their Countdown/Free Offer Days system – more about that later.) For the readers, members of Amazon Prime are automatically entitled to free downloads of KU titles. My sales plummeted overnight. I stopped enrolling new books to Amazon KDP Select and 'Went Wide' as the indie author expression goes, making ePubs for loading to Apple iBooks, Barnes & Noble, Nook etc. However, in the summer of 2015 the goalposts suddenly moved again. Amazon decided to pay library subscription royalties to authors for each page read rather than per book borrowed. If your books are of a reasonable length (ie not 'shorts') and of good quality (ie they're likely to be read until the end!) this brings about a far better KU income rate.

You can find the most recent discussions at the Kboards Writer's Cafe – the main watercooler chatroom for independent authors.
Http://www.kboards.com/

ePub The most popular open ebook format used for the Apple iBook, the (soon to be obsolete) NOOK, Sony Reader, Kobo, Adobe Digital Editions, a variety of phone e-readers and more. Amazon Kindle now take ePub (though there are, for the moment, issues and Amazon's own Mobi is still the way to go). In Jan 2013 Smashwords (see below) began accepting ePub files, bringing ePub one step closer to becoming the one-stop universal ebook formatting system.

Mobi /KF8 for KDP, the Kindle ebook system which sells on the all-powerful Amazon sales platforms. You can also load Mobi files to Kobo.

Smashwords' Multi-Format Meatgrinder a one-upload system that converts your Word doc to ePub, Mobi, PDF and more, and then distributes those files to the various selling platforms (Apple iBooks, Kobo, Barnes & Noble, Sony etc). Now that Smashwords takes ePub, this step can be skipped.

PDF more or less obsolete now as a main ebook format, but certainly has its uses. Some reviewers still request PDF copies and PDFs are still the standard format to send to international agents who might be interested in buying translation rights. If you are going to make a paperback of your book as well, this will be done as a PDF (this is why it's still the standard format in the translation rights world. See Chapter 27 – How To Grow Your Sales Through The Roof for more info on rights sales).

Putting Your Ebook Up For Sale For both Kindle and Smashwords, once you've prepared your master document you are guided through the uploading process in simple, straightforward stages. Then the ebookstores sell your ebooks for you and take a percentage of the sales price of each book. It doesn't cost anything to put your book up and royalty percentages vary. On Kindle you can keep close track of your sales, monitoring them 'live' as they happen (very addictive) and watch your rankings change accordingly. Smashwords' direct sales from their website operate in the same way. They update their statements of sale from the various outpost platforms regularly but not instantly. If you change any copy, this also takes some time to filter through to the sales pages of the ebooks on platforms other than their own.

WHERE DO YOU START?

Though Adobe PDF is fairly obsolete as a way of selling ebooks and Smashwords' own Meatgrinder system is now being usurped by ePub, I'm assuming you're going to make four SEPARATE ebook documents, all adaptations of the first Master you make for Smashwords:

1.Smashwords

2.Mobi Amazon Digital for Kindle

3.ePub

4.Adobe PDF

and that your MS (manuscript) has hyperlinks and images.

My suggested order of doing things, more detailed info to follow:

1.Smashwords First make the Smashwords version in Word (Smashwords doesn't take Open Office). Do this even if you're not going to make your ebook for Smashwords as yet, because once you've formatted your book to their precise guidelines you've also got a document that is, in computer-speak, laid out cleanly for the other ebook formats as well.

2.Mobi for Kindle To make the Kindle version, make a copy of your nice cleanly formatted Smashwords Master to use as your starting point and make the changes necessary to turn it into a Kindle Master.

3.ePub. When you have that doc prepared, a few simple further steps will also give you a document suitable for turning into an ePub Master suitable for direct loading to other sites. You can also load ePub direct to Smashwords but their technical requirements ARE a challenge and you may prefer to stick to Smashwords' own 'Meatgrinder' system. If you're not afraid of a technical challenge, Mark Binner will show you how to make a cleanly formatted ePub ebook that will get through their comprehensive check system in Chapter 28 of this book.

4.PDF Take a copy of your clean, hyperlinked ePub master to turn into your PDF Master. This can be precisely styled and designed on the page with links and photographs. Any spacings, indents, fonts, positionings, page breaks you make on the page will transfer exactly to the PDF final version.

For a more detailed, technical, explanation of ebook formats, please see Chapter 28.

PRINT ON DEMAND (POD)

Once you've made your ebook you might also consider making a PDF POD (Print on Demand) paperback. A parallel, quieter evolution than ebooks, POD is going to be just as powerful a tool for the independent author (See Chapter 8).

CHAPTER 4

LIBEL

Libel is terrifying, not least for the way it can creep up behind you from the most unexpected places. I was once told my blog was libellous for stating, in some inane by-the-by chatter, that I hadn't received a reply to a query email I'd sent out to a literary agent. Not receiving replies from query letters to literary agents isn't an infrequent occurrence but she had every right to say that. I had blackened her name and threatened her professionalism. It frightened the life out of me and I took down every word immediately.

Since then, new UK laws have come into force. It's now much more difficult to sue somebody for libel than it used to be. The Defamation Act, 2013 states that the offending words have to be shown to 'have caused or would be likely to cause serious harm to the reputation of the complainant'.

The only failsafe defence of libel is if it's the truth. You cannot be sued for libel if what you're saying is true, which is why those Kitty Kelly-type celebrity 'exposes' can get published.

As I write this, the UK newspapers are full of a landmark case showing how one remark by a journalist in one article has led to a two-year battle with costs of £200,000 $291,000: http://www.guardian.co.uk/commentisfree/libertycentral/2010/apr/02/simon-singh-help-me-win-libel-reform

This is an area where self-publishers really are at a disadvantage. Publishing house editors know what to look out for and can refer anything they're not totally sure about to their lawyers. The work may also already have been read by an experienced literary agent with half of one eye trained on the legal ball.

A copy editor may flag up a problem area but the buck rests firmly with you. It's solely down to you to check, check and double-check.

CHAPTER 5

TITLES, ISBNs, LEGAL NOTICES AND DISCLAIMERS

The big words at the front and the little words at the beginning and end.

Titles

When my ex-agent was considering whether to take on my latest novel or not, her main concern was the title. It wasn't until I'd suggested 5 or 6 titles (out of a shortlist of dozens) that I found one that she thought was good enough and she signed me up.

If I hadn't come up with a great title I wouldn't have been taken on. Period.

I even had an agent contact me once who'd been given a title by an editor at one of the major publishing houses. She was looking for an author to write the book to fit it.

That's how important a title is.

Give it a lot of thought.

In October 2014 I changed the title of this book from *How To Publish An Ebook On A Budget* to *Self-Publishing Ebooks* because self-publishing ebooks is one of the top Google searches for the subject. By having the words opening my title line my book stands a better chance of being discovered. Opening with "How To" is also a lost opportunity – they are dead words that don't relate to the subject. Find out what search terms are popular around your subject by going to Google Analytics Key Words and Google Trends.

Ask the opinions of those around you but don't drive them crazy. Invite a group of friends round for wine and food and a one-off brainstorming session. If you belong to a writing group, give one of your reading slots up to a title search.

Here's a list of book titles taken from literature: http://bit.ly/1u5Qzh5

ISBNs

Every print book that's sold in a shop and/or stored in a public library has to have an ISBN number and bar code. ISBN stands for the International Standard Book Number. The ISBN registration agency, run in the UK by Nielsen, and in the US by Bowker, reaches out to over 100 countries around the world.

You can purchase your own ISBN if you want to give your book an identity but you have to buy them in batches of 10 which costs £132.00 in the UK.

http://www.isbn.nielsenbook.co.uk/controller.php?page=123

In the US you can purchase an individual ISBN from Bowker for $125, or buy 10 for $275.

http://www.bowker.com/en-US/products/servident_isbn.shtml

The good news is that ebooks don't need them at all. There are advantages, they're necessary for print books which will be listed in the bookshop and library catalogues around the world, but you don't have to have one.

If you publish with an ePublishing site, some of them allocate a free ISBN which will list that company as the book's publisher. You don't need to worry about this, you still hold all the copyright and are free to register the book with other ePublishers. The same book can be published as a print version with a free CreateSpace ISBN. The only restriction is that some sites have a pricing policy. Amazon Kindle, for example, says that your list price mustn't be greater than the lowest retail price for any physical edition of your book. If your ebook is priced lower anywhere else, their terms and conditions state they will lower the price on their site. They don't need to inform you, it will just happen.

If you do decide to assign an ISBN to your ebook, each different version (ePub, Kindle, PDF etc) will require a different ISBN. If you are republishing a book of yours that has been published in print before, DON'T use the ISBN number. See the Smashwords summary of ISBNs and ebooks: http://www.smashwords.com/dashboard/ISBNManager/.

Disclaimers

If you've written a novel, you'll need to insert the all persons are fictitious disclaimer.

If you have included people you know, even if it's just their name as an in joke, email them to ask their permission first. Even if it's your best friend, closest relative and it's the most flattering portrait in the world, situations do change.

If you've written a non-fiction book, the easiest way to see if you've covered every angle in the disclaimers section is go to a bookshop or library, find a title that covers a similar area and see what their publishers have written at the front.

My very first ebook, *Done & Dusted: The Organic Home on a Budget*, has lots of advice on cleaning and stain removal so I had to make it clear that I would not be liable for any damage or loss resulting from anybody following the advice in the book.

I was once asked by a newspaper reader if they could tell me if they had a legal case against a chair manufacturer after they'd spilled something on the cover which wouldn't come out. I refused to answer the question or they might have shifted their legal claim over to me. Some people are just extremely litigious and authors and self-publishers can't be too careful in covering themselves.

Here's what I have in the front of *Done & Dusted: First published by Blackbird Digital Books LONDON*
© Stephanie Zia 2010. All rights reserved.
The cleaning and stains problems addressed in this book and their solutions are universal, but please be aware that this book was written in the UK. Where

23

products and websites are concerned, there is, therefore, an unavoidable UK bias. No refunds can be given on this basis. US prices and websites have been included wherever possible. All prices and exchange rates quoted are liable to fluctuation and change at any time. They may or may not include taxes, postage and packing and the reader must check with each individual linked website. Updates will be included in subsequent editions. Rough US dollar equivalents are given to sterling wherever possible. While the information and advice in this ebook are believed to be accurate and true at the time of publication, neither the author, publisher or distributor can guarantee results nor accept any responsibility or liability for any damage or losses of any kind resulting from any advice included in this guide, be it from the author, any person or persons mentioned in this guide, or any product, listing or mention, whether directly or indirectly. Successful treatments and savings are the responsibility of the reader of this book.

If the contents of your ebook are controversial in any way and you're getting sleepless nights about whether you should publish or not, there is professional liability insurance but it's not cheap. Even at the reduced rate the cost is likely to be around £500/$728 per annum in the UK and more in the US.

Check carefully to see what you're covered for. There are lots of insurance companies that sell policies for writers which include public liability and legal costs if you pursue your own case but the policy (especially if it's suspiciously cheap) may well not cover you if anybody sues you.

The US Author's Guild has a package for its members which covers libel, slander or disparagement; invasion of privacy; trademark and copyright infringements and plagiarism.

CHAPTER 6

HOW TO MAKE YOUR EBOOK FOR SMASHWORDS, APPLE IBOOKS, & MORE

'If you ignore the formatting requirements of the Smashwords
Style Guide, Meatgrinder will turn your book into hamburger.
Please follow the instructions!'
Mark Coker, founder & CEO, Smashwords

Smashwords is a central ebook-making and sales platform. You only have to download your formatted text once (either your original Word or in an ePub format that you've already made). If you load in Word, they'll turn your words into ePub along with all the eformats that serve the different types of ereader, computer and/or mobile phone (but not, as yet, for retail on Amazon Kindle). The same happens if you load in ePub, which is better because you have more control over the final look of your book – spacings etc – before you get to the loading stage.

You set the retail price and purchasers can buy your ebook direct from Smashwords or from the ebookreaders' own catalogues. These include: Stanza; Sony Reader; Palm Doc; Apple iBookstore; Kobo; Apps and more. Smashwords' ebook creation services are free, all copyrights remain with you. They take a cut of your sales before forwarding your royalties to PayPal.

Smashwords is a good place to start, even if you've decided to make a Kindle-only version to start with (to take advantage of Amazon's exclusivity deals), because the basic formatting guide you follow will give you a good, clean Master Word document to make copies of to adjust for independent ePub loading, Mobi for Amazon and PDF for paperback.

Smashwords describe themselves as *'ideal for publishing novels, short fiction, poetry, personal memoirs, monographs, non-fiction, research reports, essays, or other written forms that haven't even been invented yet'* . Texts that have anything other than straightforward spacing requirements, modern poetry for example, can be a challenge.

You have complete control over the sampling, pricing and marketing of your written works. Founder Mark Coker is one of the heroes of independent publishing. He has an interesting story to tell of his own journey trying to get into mainstream publishing not dissimilar to my own experiences with my fiction.

Mark has produced two helpful How To books, dowload from Smashwords:

The Smashwords Style Guide (free) The Smashwords Style Guide makes it easy to format your manuscript to produce high quality multi-format ebooks.

Smashwords Book Marketing Guide (free) How to market your books on Smashwords. How Smashwords helps promote your book, and 26 simple do-it-yourself marketing tips.

Mark's instructions are clear, well-written and easy to understand and put into practice.

Pros: Smashwords is brilliant. It's free. Your book is sold to an instant worldwide market. Very few style problems for works that have no special spacing requirements.

You only have to load one master document and Smashwords will digitise and ship your ebooks. For this reason, from now on I will umbrella Barnes & Noble, Sony, Apple iBooks etc under the Smashwords title.

Cons: Now that Smashwords accepts ePub, a lot of the Cons have – potentially – disappeared. However it's a challenge to get your formatted ePub book past the strict Smashwords Techie Requirements. Techie guidelines on how to do this are at the end of this book in Chapter 28. If you choose to use their, simpler, Meatgrinder method, diagrams and illustrations are OK but not tables (this goes for all ebooks though this system is the least stable). As the one Word document is converted to multiple formats, with Meatgrinder you don't have close control on how your ebook will look over all the platforms until it's there and spacings can be tricky. You can get a good idea by previewing the Smashwords version before publishing. To balance this, updating your document after it's been published and then reloading is simple and efficient. You can also preview your Smashwords ebook on the free Adobe Digital Editions ePub ebook viewer. You can do a test run without making the book 'live'.

There are publication cons once your book is published. It can take time to make changes: if you want to change the price or take the book down altogether it can be a very frustrating and long-winded process to get the information through to all the different platforms. For this reason I now sell my non-exclusive ebooks through Draft2Digital (see below).

Selling on Smashwords

Opting in and out of the various markets Smashwords offers you is simple. The Smashwords storefront is instant after upload. Though it takes time for them to get your multiformatted ebook out to the different stores (anything up to 8 weeks), your one document upload to Smashwords will get your ebook retailing in the Apple iBookstore (expanding all the time, reaches over 50 countries), Sony, Apple, the Diesel eBook Store, Kobo, Borders, Stanza, Aldiko, FBReader and Word-Player, Borders Australia, Angus & Robertson Australia, Whitcoulls (New Zealand) and more. Though Smashwords don't as yet distribute to Amazon, they produce ebooks in the Mobi format so that purchasers can read an ebook purchased from them on their Kindles.

The above was correct at the time of writing. Advances in the downloading technology are happening fast and Mark stays ahead of the game so check out the Smashwords blog and Smashwords Site Updates for the latest information: http://blog.smashwords.com/

Another Pro: The Smashwords Coupon Code system is useful for sending free review copies to potential reviewers (Kindle format is catered for), for giving competition prizes and for discounts to friends and bloggers. At Blackbird Digital Books we negotiated a free download code offer with a national organisation for our first children's book, *The Dream Theatre*, by Sarah Ball using a specially-created Smashwords code and have used this method for blog and magazine competitions.

Now to get making your Master ebook document **If you're going to make an ePub to load to Smashwords, follow the Style Guide and instructions below but KEEP hyperlinks and KEEP chapter page breaks.**

The *Smashwords Style Guide* (free): https://www.smashwords.com/books/view/52 gives you all the information you need on how to prepare your basic Smashwords Meatgrinder ebook document.

Though Smashwords now takes ePub files, following the formatting guidelines is still an excellent way to start. This will also become the cleanly formatted Master which you will then adapt for your other Masters. Instructions on images and how to add them come later in this book. The Style Guide is regularly updated so always read the latest, online, version.

You have to make your Smashwords Master in Microsoft Word .doc format (Maximum file size 5MB).

The fonts recommended for Smashwords documents are Times New Roman, Garamond or Arial (size 14 maximum). To get into the Premium Catalogue, font sizes must remain small, 12pt is preferred with a maximum of 16pt for headings. The fonts recommended for Amazon Kindle documents are Times New Roman, Arial or Georgia (size 12, 14 maximum). The fonts are converted in the machinery anyway so if you're making both ebooks it makes sense to use TNR or Arial.

The two major differences between a Smashwords Meatgrinder document and your other Masters is that it's a continuous text and it doesn't take hyperlinks. Page breaks that automatically appear on your Word or Open Office document are irrelevant. This is important to realise when it comes to headings. It's tempting to click down a space or so if a heading comes at the bottom of a page, for example. So, if one line of a heading is at the bottom of one page, the second line on top of the next, ignore it. Think of Jack Kerouac writing *On The Road,* which he did on a series of continuous rolls of paper, a bit like writing on toilet rolls.

Remember that the document you are preparing will be uploaded once to the Smashwords Meatgrinder where it will thence be processed and distributed to a wide variety of different ebook reading formats. The key to a successful layout and presentation, therefore, is to KEEP IT SIMPLE! The Meatgrinder doesn't take tabs, tables, footnotes, text in columns or text boxes. Special fonts and anything other than straightforward indents or spacings will not work. Hyperlinks to websites will also be rejected. If you want to tell your readers about a link, write it out in full using the http:// at the beginning. Don't have lots of different fonts, spacings or indent styles. Italics and (low res) colour images will work. Avoid Headings and Bold. Whilst bold text may work on some ePub conversions, others will fail to read properly and your ebook will come out with a nasty patchwork of bold paragraphs all over the place.

If you find text that isn't formatting properly when you download your final ePub version for checking: highlight that text, move it to Text Edit/Notepad and make it into Plain Text before cutting and pasting it back into the document.

If you have more than four spacings in a row, the Meatgrinder will read 'blank page' and create a blank page in the middle of your text.

If you are using images there is a file upload limit of 5MB (this will be explained later in the *Working With Photographs and Images* section).

Indents are the biggest trip-up point. Paragraph indents are the main formatting error that gets your book rejected for the all-important Smashwords Premium Catalogue. If you are writing a novel, use the ruler bar at the top of your document to make a space indent at the beginning of every paragraph. DON'T use the tab key or the space bar to create indents or your book will be rejected. If you are using block paragraphs DON'T use the space bar to make a gap between paragraphs. Instead go to FORMAT > Paragraph and in Spacing put 6pt in the 'After' column (graphics to explain in the Style Guide) and use the carriage return key. To find any rogue line spacings, look for backward P thingys on their own after a paragraph. A paragraph that has been 6pt marked will not have a backward P between the spacings.

The main problem I had with formatting for both PDF and ePublishing sites was that paragraphs would do sudden leaps forwards, or gaps between line-spacings would, for some strange reason, be twice as wide as they looked on the page.

One of Mark Coker's major, major tips I so wish, wished I'd known about before making my ebook is this: Make Word's paragraph/spacing etc instructions VISIBLE ON THE PAGE.

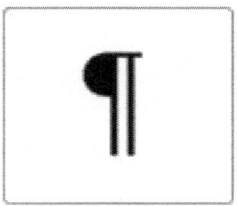

All you do is click on what Mark Coker calls 'the reverse P thingy' in your Word toolbar (see how wonderfully non teccy he is?) and, hey presto, you can see where all the glitches and wrong spaces are and eliminate them. If you can't see it in your toolbar, the official name for this symbol is the Pilcrow. (In Open Office, which Smashwords doesn't accept, but for reference if you''re using it for other versions, as I do for the paperback, the backward P is hidden in: VIEW > Non-Printing Characters.) Writing new text with these marks visible could easily put you off your stride, so start off with them visible for the first few paragraphs. This way you'll make sure that you're not getting into any bad habits. Then click on the backwards P again to make the markings disappear, and then add them again at the editing stage.

The mysterious spaces and leaps that creep into your final document happen in the formatting process where you hit the tab button and carriage return buttons. It's all explained in the guide.

I used to always use the Nuclear Formatting Option suggested in the Style Guide. This removes any hidden spacing trip-wires hidden in the page layout of your creative document that you've revised, deleted, cut and pasted into and all the rest. This way you start off with a squeaky clean, glitch-free Master document that you can also use for making your Kindle and PDF Masters. However, if you are converting only to .Mobi for Kindle on Calibre it is possible to sometimes skip this step without any problems. If you do skip this step and discover spacing problems when you do your first test conversion, 'nuking' may then be the solution you need.

To 'nuke' your document, highlight all the text on your finished master manuscript (having made a safety copy first!) and cut and paste it to Notepad (PC) or TextEdit (Mac, called SimpleText on earlier Macs).

Then take out all the hidden computer formatting codes by turning the text into SimpleText (sometimes called Plain Text).

FORMAT > Make Plain Text

Then transfer the SimpleText to a fresh blank Word document. This will ensure that you're starting off on nice clean pages with nice clean words where there are no hidden cache's to trip you up later.

Paragraph Spacings and Indents

For a professional look, use single spacing with no spaces between paragraphs. Indent each paragraph slightly (noting that the indent is often exaggerated in the final ebook transfer process) EXCEPT for the first line of every chapter which should be blocked to the L.

Images on Smashwords

There's a maximum upload limit of 5MB. The Style Guide shows you how to compress your images in Word to their recommended 96dpi. Detailed information on photos and photo sizing comes later in this book.

If you find it's all beyond you, Mark also tells you how to get in touch with authors who'll format your document for you for about $30/ £21 an hour.

Epub Without Smashwords

The simplest way to make your own ePub file is via the free (donations requested) ebook management system Calibre, http://calibre-ebook.com/. It's a straightforward procedure and, as long as you're using the most up-to-date download of Calibre, you should have few problems. Older versions (the only kind you can download on the older Macs) produce some formatting problems. If, like me, you have an old Mac, don't bother with Calibre for Mac but instead borrow a friend's up-to-date Mac or a PC to carry out the transfer. Once you've familiarised yourself with the process this can be done in a few minutes. I have a PC laptop which I use for Calibre (and also for Kindle previewing). The other simple transfer option is the novelists's software package: http://www.literatureandlatte.com/scrivener.php/. Scrivener was originally formulated for Macs and would probably be a more stable option. It costs $40 but there's a generous free trial if you want to try it out.

If you have a book that isn't straight text, or straight text/image layout, and are familiar with HTML computer code, or are willing to learn, you might want to have a go at formatting your ePub book yourself. Read Mark Binner's advanced techie guidelines in Chapter 28. One of the top recommendations is Guido Henkel's online guide for beginners http://guidohenkel.com/2010/12/take-pride-in-your-ebook-formatting/

You do have to be able to follow technical instructions for Guido's guide, and certainly take no notice of his opening paragraph which is very unflattering about authors' efforts at doing it for themselves. With the help of Smashwords you can produce excellent ePub books without having to go into all the HTML detail. Tens of thousands have already done so and that's the proof of it.

Apple offers a self-publishing option on iBooks. You can do this already very well for free via Smashwords and I gather the Apple route isn't that straightforward. For starters, if you're offering your book for sale (rather than putting it out for free) you will need to purchase an ISBN (not needed for ebooks generally). I also gather you need to have access to a modern Mac computer. Please see Chapter 28, where Mark Binner will take you through all the main techie options. If you don't know about HTML but want a good basic beginner's guide, there are some brilliant tutorial link recommendations here as well.

Draft2Digital
https://www.draft2digital.com/.
An (also free to access) alternative to Smashwords: For both ease of uploading material, and, more importantly, ease of taking down material and changing the prices. These can take a while with Smashwords and when you need to be flexible to keep up with whatever publishing incentives crop up next, this is a Big Plus. As at January 2015 I'm thinking of leaving KDP Select and distributing to non-Amazon retailers through this system instead.

Bookbaby For around $149, the US site Bookbaby http://www.bookbaby.com/ will convert your document to ePub and Mobi ebooks and put them up on to Amazon, iBooks, Barnes & Noble etc for you. You then pay an annual fee of around $19 but you get to keep 100% of any royalties earned.

Sigil http://code.google.com/p/sigil/ is a free shareware systems that operate on a voluntary donation basis. Good for fine-tuning. Works on both PC and (newish!) Macs and, though technical, is logically set out and navigable for the non-techie (but not recommended for the complete beginner).

Some General Handy Computer Hints:

CTRL (OR APPLE) + Z = Deletes last command. Very useful if you find your page suddenly turning into a maze of indents and spacings.

EDIT (running across top of screen) + SELECT ALL = highlights all the text at once.

SAVING FILES – You'll probably find yourself saving several versions of the same document. It's very easy to get them muddled up. Make a habit of always saving files with a number at the beginning. For this book, for example, I'm saving my documents as ebookbudget, 2ebookbudget, 3ebookbudget, etc. When you have the version number at the beginning you can immediately pick out the latest version from the linear presentation of documents.

FORMATTING HELL – If words get stuck, paragraphs refuse to move or underlined lines will not de-underline themselves, try highlighting the problem area and clicking:
In Word: FORMAT > Clear Formatting.
In Open Office: FORMAT > Default Formatting.
'TEXT BODY' WINDOW Top left. Another way to shift stubborn formatting is to highlight the problem area, open the drop-down menu and select 'clear formatting' .

THE PAINTBRUSH! There's a little paintbrush in the Toolbar called the 'Format Paintbrush' . This is very useful if you get text that stubbornly refuses to budge or space correctly for no apparent reason. The reason is hidden formatting. Highlight the area, click on the brush and 'paint' over it to remove hidden formatting.

SAVE YOUR MASTER DOCUMENTS AFTER EVERY WRITING SESSION – If your computer isn't linked to an online document saving system (a 'cloud') or a separate back-up hard drive, get Dropbox – https://www.dropbox.com/ – a fantastic free online file sync, file sharing and backup software. Saves your work and makes it accessible online from any computer.

CURLY QUOTES To change 'straight quotes' to, the generally preferred, more professional-looking, 'curly quotes' in Word go to Tools > AutoCorrect. Under 'Replace As You Type' , select the "Straight quotes" with "smart quotes" check box. Then, to replace a whole document, highlight all the text and then and click Auto Correct.

SPACING BETWEEN LINES To make spaces between lines that will convert to formatting language, go to PAGE LAYOUT (Word) FORMAT (Open Office), then PARAGRAPH > and then add a measurement to Spacing Above Paragraph and/or Spacing Below Paragraph. As a guide, 0.30cm is used generally throughout this document. Spaces made as you type normally, by hitting the Enter key twice for example, which brings up a backward P space, won't convert.

CHAPTER 7

HOW TO MAKE A MASTER DOCUMENT FOR AMAZON KINDLE MOBI , DRAFT2DIGITAL AND KOBO EPUB

To make your Kindle Mobi and ePub ebooks separately (free), you use a copy of the same Word master document you made for Smashwords with a few small adjustments. You then transfer this to Mobi via Calibre for upload to Amazon's KDP (Kindle Direct Publishing) sales site and to ePub via Calibre for other independent ePub sales platforms like Draft2Digital (a one-stop load that covers Apple, Kobo and more), Kobo direct or (if you're a technical whizz) direct to Smashwords.

First, take a look at the official Kindle guides:If you have more than a little technical knowledge, you can find Amazon's 78-page free download PDF, *Publishing on Kindle: Guidelines for Publishers* at Kindle Publishing Guidelines http://amzn.to/VRP214

Otherwise the simpified guide, *Building Your Book For Kindle*, from Word in both PC and Mac available free from the Amazon Kindle Store. Their instructions on how to make a clickable TOC, Table of Contents, for Kindle are clarified and simplified later in this book.

Amazon recommends using KDP's free Kindle Previewer, KindleGen, to make your ebook. As my Mac is too old to take

KindleGen, I can't give direct instructions on how to use this, but I can say that, if the forums are anything to go by, it's probably not worth the effort.

It is possible to load Word or HTML direct to Amazon KDP, but with the advent of the more technically complex Kindle Fire ereader, it has really become necessary to load the more robustly hardwired Mobi file if you don't want to get customer complaints. For some reason best known to themselves, for example, some people like to read white text on a black screen, this will not work if your Master has been loaded as an HTML or Word document.

I have always found using Calibre by far the easiest, most robust, method of producing Mobi (and ePub) files. (People who have Scrivener writing software also vouch for its ease of use.) If you then want to make fine code adjustments, there is a free ePub software called Sigil, but that is a techie area and not needed for straightforward conversions.

Epub for Kindle is a no-no at the moment as the table of contents doesn't convert. PDF for Kindle has never worked properly.

If you have made a Smashwords Master Word document, make a copy of it to use as your Kindle Master. Rename it clearly straight away so that you don't get confused when you have to re-open files later. (Open the Smashwords document. Click FILE > Save As then type: KINDLEMaster-titleofbook) If you are not making a Smashwords Master document, follow all the formatting instructions for making a Smashwords Master noting that – The two main differences between a Smashwords and Kindle Master document are: You're now going to format to the semi-toilet-roll system rather than the full toilet-roll system. The opening title will be on its own separate page, as will the publisher information etc etc. But when you're into a chapter you revert to the continuous rolling text method, ie, don't space the words to the page, if a page overlaps between a heading and its subject, don't put in any carriage return spaces to make it look better. Once it's in the Mobi system, the text will all run together, following its own page breaks unrelated to your document page breaks. For this reason don't leave anything but the smallest space between headings and the text below or they could, in the final formatted document, turn out to have a wider gap than intended.

Unlike Smashwords' Meatgrinder, Kindle documents can take hyperlinks to exterior websites. Website links (if any) typed out in full in your Smashwords document can now be hyperlinked. (See Chapter 10 – A Beginner's Guide to Hyperlinking) You don't have to present your document in a particular font as it will convert automatically. There's no point wasting time trying out other fonts because they will just get transferred back to the Kindle defaults. So write your document in one of the approved fonts – Times New Roman, Arial or Georgia.

Follow the Simple Formatting Guide:Space out your title and book frontispiece informationOne page for title and author New page for publisher information New page for disclaimers etc

New page for Contents

Take out the Smashwords references, if used, at the frontInsert page breaks between each blank frontispiece page and between each chapter: WORD – Insert > Break > Page Break[OPEN OFFICE – Insert > Manual Break > Page Break > OK]IMAGES More about images later but as a general round-up:

Images Within The Book

If your document has images, you could, until recently, load straight to Kindle as a WORD document. It's still possible to do this but is not to be recommended any more because issues could arise for Kindle Fire readers. If you have a more modern computer you will have a SAVE AS HTML FILTERED option for your document. Sometimes called SAVE AS WEB PAGE FILTERED option, this will convert images. Sometimes it hasn't worked for me so always double check the images are there before publishing. Though you can load the HTML file for publication, for greater stability it's best to convert this HTML file to Mobi.

At the time of writing, images inside your Kindle document can be in GIF, PNG, BMP or Jpeg. The Kindle book format supports JPEG and GIF image files up to 5MB. Size your images at 520 pixels x 640 pixels. Check for updates at Formatting Images Within Your Kindle Book: https://kdp.amazon.com/self-publishing/help?topicId=A1B6GKJ79HC7AN Graphic, line images reproduce better in GIF. Jpeg is the most commonly used image type.

If your pictures aren't converted to a tiny size you'll find that, whatever size you make them on your Word master, in conversion they'll blow up to full Kindle page size. This leaves no room for text. Not even for a heading.

To fix this right click the picture and select 'FORMAT PICTURE' Select 'SIZE' from the horizontal menu running across the top of the pop-up window.

Make the width about 4.90cm, the height will then come out at about 3.7cm (this will vary slightly depending on the size of your Master). Click OK.

If you work out how to use KindleGen, you can upload the highest quality picture files you have (preferably at 300dpi). They will be adjusted to the maximum quality available. This is called futureproofing. As improvements in the image quality of Kindle come along in the future, your images will be automatically upgraded to the maximum quality.

Extra step to take if you have lots of images
Whilst Amazon accept ebook sizes up to 5MB, a large Kindle file with lots of images will cost more to send to a customer and reduce your profits. This can be addressed by compressing all of your pictures, reducing the pixel count, which won't make any visible difference at all on the small ereader screens.

This can be done on all your pictures with a few clicks. In Word, click on any of your images. Go to

Format > Picture Tools

Go to the Adust section > Compress Pictures

Uncheck the box "Apply only to this picture". Check the box "Use document resolution" is ticked. > OK.

Transfer

When your Word document is ready, transfer it to HTML by clicking 'Save As' , then select 'Web Page' or it may be labelled 'HTML' . Some set-ups will have a 'Filtered HTML' 'Filtered Web Page' option. Select this one. Esp important if you have photographs in your book as unfiltered HTML won't reproduce images.

You now have a document ready for conversion to Mobi via Calibre (or Scrivener). The Mobi file will be made in the same single Calibre process described below for making an ePub file. Follow all the steps through and when it comes to pressing the 'convert to ePub' you'll see also the option to 'convert to Mobi' . Both files will transfer to your desktop ready for checking before loading to the sales platforms.

Cover Image

You will need to make a cover image for the sales page and for your promotions.

KDP takes Jpeg or TIFF files for covers. The recommended size for cover art is 1563 x 2500 pixels. Save at 72dpi (more about all these terms later). The preferred height/width ratio is 1:6. Images smaller than 625 x 1000 will be rejected. Your cover is loaded as a separate file and is then incorporated automatically into your main Kindle document when you upload. If you are making a paperback as well, start off with a high quality cover image at 300dpi which can be reduced to a smaller 72dpi for the ebook.

MAKE A SEPARATE EPUB EBOOK

We're doing this here because the Kindle Word doc more closely resembles the standard ePub Master than the Smashwords Word doc. Two main reasons: direct hyperlinks to the internet are allowed in Kindle, not in Smashwords; page separation is required in Kindle, not in Smashwords. The ePub you make can be used generally anywhere an ePub is required, for selling from Kobo, your website, etc.

Make a new copy of your Kindle Word document and label it TitleofBook-ePubMaster.doc.

Go through the text and take out any references that you may have in your front and back idents which refer to Amazon. You may be asking readers to kindly think about reviewing your book on Amazon, for example. If this is left in on a Smashwords ePub Master, they will, understandably, reject your book. If you are making the ePub for Kobo, you may want to ask readers to leave reviews on the Kobo website.

Make sure your chapter listings are listed straight through from beginning to end with no breaks. This book, for example, is divided into four parts. My original index was divided by these part separations. This threw up an almighty storm when it came to the ePub reader trying to decipher chapter separation in its Table of Contents and the whole thing crashed. So make sure the chapter listing at the front of your document reads simply all the way through: 1,2,3 etc.

Save as HTML Web Page filtered.

See Chapter 22 for step by step instructions on how to convert this document to your final Mobi and ePub files on Calibre.

CHAPTER 8

HOW TO MAKE YOUR PDF EBOOK AND SOME POD, PAPERBACK, GUIDELINES

PDF is the earliest form of ebook. Since the rise of the Kindle, iBook, etc this style of simple PDF for ebooks has waned. You can make Adobe PDF ebooks from start to finish on your computer, no special online ebook formatting system required. Adobe itself is now using the ePub format. However, basic home Adobe makes excellent, full colour ebooks and is still very much in use for making paperbacks, online brochures, leaflets etc. The design software used by virtually all professionals is Adobe InDesign® which retails at £ 699.12/$1009. This is the system used for making print books. You will use the free version of Adobe PDF if you decide to make POD (print on demand) paperbacks to sell on Amazon alongside your ebooks. PDF documents can be read on computers, mobile phones, iPads and iPods. They can be transferred to a few eReaders, some (eg Sony Reader) more successfully than others, but are pretty much over (for now, see below).

Pros: Free. All done offline at your computer. Looks good. Easy to insert photographs and diagrams. You have total control of the final look of your book – cover, spacings, fonts, styles, layouts etc. Perfect for distribution yourself ie selling from your own website; sending to friends and relatives. Perfect for making POD

(' print on demand') paperbacks plus pamphlets, flyers etc to promote your ebooks.

Cons: Not versatile. Not commercial. You can't successfully transfer the finished document to the big ebook selling sites like Amazon Kindle and the rest unless you're using the pro InDesign system. In which case Kindle Plugin for Adobe InDesign® is a free plug-in which can be used to convert documents or books created in Adobe InDesign® to Kindle format. The free Adobe system has progressed from a simple desktop viewing system to a comprehensive ePub ebook software: Adobe Digital Editions. Download free: http://www.adobe.com/uk/products/digital-editions.html?autoPrompt=true/. Use it to read Adobe Ebooks in ePub format (on a lovely, book-like page-turning interface), and transfer Adobe Ebooks onto many ebook reader/phone/computer screens. A development in process is ePub 3.0. Ebooks produced in this format will be able to support multimedia content such as video, audio and much more. A child can colour in a picture and email it to their parents for example. The gossip is that the digital wizardry preserve of the App (expensive to produce/hard to make a profit on as retail prices are so low) will be challenged.

First take your Kindle Master document, make a copy and rename it PDF Master. Then, check that it will transfer to PDF.

Click on FILE at the very top of your s creen and see if there is an EXPORT TO PDF option. Most versions of Word have this, but if yours is as old as mine and there isn't that option, these are free converters you can download: http://www.primopdf.com/ is recommended by reader Michael McMahon. Or try CutePDF http://www.cutepdf.com/Products/CutePDF/writer.asp/.

OR if you don't intend making a Word Master for Smashwords and/or Kindle and are only making a PDF you could make your master on Open Office. An open-source (ie free) word processing package that, like Word, includes graphics, databases, spreadsheets etc. You can use it on PCs and Macs for any purpose, domestic, commercial, educational etc. It doesn't replace your Word system but works alongside it so you can have

Word and Open Office files stored in the same folder with no problems. Reader Mark Binner has pointed out that there is also the option to use LibreOffice, an increasingly popular fork of OpenOffice. LibreOffice is, he says, updated more frequently. Kingsoft is also a fantastic free word-processing package.

I made my first PDF from scratch in Open Office. The OO help pages are comprehensive but I found them to be slightly more geeky than I was used to. Its graphics package is particularly impressive but became my undoing when I (temporarily as it turned out) lost all my images.

With Adobe PDF you have a wide choice of fonts but don't go over the top. Many of the fancy fonts won't work well on transfer.

Do a test page of a paragraph per font and transfer the page to PDF and have a look.

Start with the fonts that are recommended for uploading to Amazon Kindle: Times New Roman, Arial, Georgia. Use a standard size 12, 14 maximum.

I chose to make my PDF ebooks in Arial narrow, size 14. The chapter headings are the same font in bold, size 18.

Don't be tempted to mix fonts. Unless you know what you're doing, mixing font styles can easily look amateurish. For the same reason, use colour sparingly. I used one colour for chapter and insert headings and put a narrow frame around my stills in the same colour.

If you use more than one font style on a cover (as a rule, professionals don't use more than 2) make one a Serif and one a Sans-serif. Sans-serif are the straight, bold letters (like Arial), Serif fonts have stylised twists and edges to the letters (like Times New Roman). Most cover titles are in Serif.

Indents

If you want to start every paragraph with a margin indent do it by setting up the tabulation table with the ruler at the top of your document. If you do any indents 'manually' by pressing the space bar until you get to the place you want your word to appear, you'll find that when you transfer your document there will be funny leaps and gaps where you don't want them.

To make the margins on the right into a straight, justified format rather than ragged typing, click Edit > Select All > then click the series of 4 straight lines in the main Toolbar.

Page Breaks

The PDF version is similar to your Kindle Master. The main difference is the spacing. There's no toilet roll system involved within chapters. With Adobe PDF everything transfers just as you see it on your Word or Open Office document. So take your Kindle Master and space out the words as you'd like to see them on the page.

Publishing

To transfer your Word or Open Office document to PDF see Chapter 19 – *Publishing to Adobe PDF*.

SOME POD PAPERBACK GUIDELINES

The new technology means that you can make a PDF paperback book template, very similar to your ebook template, and offer paperback versions of your book for sale on your website or through the major online channels and bookstores. POD stands for Print On Demand. No more costly bulk print orders needed. No more warehouse storage. No more pulping. No more shelling out to dubious vanity publishing companies to get a real book in your hands.

The basic system is free for authors on sites such as www.lulu.com, and (my much preferred) Amazon POD system CreateSpace www.createspace.com. IngramSpark is the pro way. Ingram will distribute your book worldwide and make it accessible for bookshop and library ordering. https://www.ingramspark.com

There are up-front costs (\$49/£29), plus you must purchase an ISBN (from Bowker in the US \$125 each or \$275 for 10; Nielsen in the UK, only available in blocks of 10 at £135), but the whole process is user-friendly and the books do become part of the mainstream distribution system. I am in the process of making my books available on IngramSpark, I thought the reality would be that no bookshop would order a copy unless it was asked to do so by a reader. But, by copying the mainstream publishers and offering the bookstores their expected 55% discount, the option to return books (tick 'return & destroy' box) orders are coming in. I even have a book on a main Waterstones display shelf, and two Waterstones 'events' in process, which is beyond all expectations. Whilst the interior file part of it was straightforward, with my original CreateSpace Master only needing an ISBN number update with my new Nielsen ISBN, I did have to go to a designer to get the cover formatted to their specifications.

CreateSpace books won't be accepted by bookstores in the UK, postage and packing charges are on the high side, the discounts aren't big enough and there's no returns option, but they are fully integrated into Amazon's sales platforms. Which is why you need to do both.

Why I Prefer Open Office For POD Paperbacks

I prefer to make my PDF POD Masters on Open Office rather than Word. This is because it's so much simpler (once you know how!) to number the pages whilst keeping the opening set of pages clean and without numbers, as is the paperback tradition. To do this place the mouse cursor at the bottom of the page where you want your numbering to begin (usually the first page of Chapter 1). Then click

INSERT>FIELD>OTHER. Then, from the menu on the pop-up window click PAGE. Where it says OFFSET at the bottom right of the menu insert the MINUS FIGURE for the number of pages at the front you want to leave blank, ie for this book there are 12 pages without numbers at the front, so in that window I type [minus] -12. Page number will now start 12 pages into the document. (I can't tell you how long it took me to find this out!)

Though American Trade 6in x 8in is recommended I prefer the 5.5in x 8.5in size for books under 80,000 words. If you'll be commissioning a cover with a cover designer, bear in mind the size of the paperback and commission the size (and ask for 300dpi) accordingly.

You get a choice of cream or white paper, cream is standard for fiction. CreateSpace has a built in 'cover creator'. You can transfer your own front cover .jpg image, a full PDF designed by a designer, or use one of their basic (not very lovely) templates. It's a completely free way of getting your books printed and out there selling. This is a whole other subject that's growing almost as rapidly as ebooks.

I was, I have to say, shocked at a POD presentation I attended at the London Book Fair a few years ago. No names, but the company was a vanity company pretending they weren't a vanity company. Whilst the London Book Fair is now a very author-friendly place, beware of online vanity publishers in disguise. Absolute Write is a good place to look at forums on user experiences.

(http://www.absolutewrite.com/forums/showthread.php?t=80048%22%20\t%20%22_top).

David Gaughran's warnings about Author Solutions are a Must Read on this subject: http://davidgaughran.wordpress.com.

CHAPTER 9

WHY YOU DON'T NEED PAGE NUMBERING

Don't put page numbers in ebooks.

Every format you'll transfer to will have its own inbuilt page numbering system.

For every system your words will fill a different size of page-space. Adobe for instance, lists its page numbers at the top or at the side of the document.

The chapter headings at the beginning of your book are hyperlinked within the document to the relevant chapter. So you click on the heading you want to read and you're instantly taken to the page (see Chapters 10 and 11 coming up).

CHAPTER 10

A BEGINNER'S GUIDE TO HYPERLINKING

Hyperlinking is when a word is underlined or highlighted so that when you click on that word you're taken to the website, or document page, it's referring to.

A basic, but not everybody knows how to do this. I'd been blogging for an embarrassing amount of time before I found out how to do it. For ages I didn't know you could have more than one internet page up on the screen at once (With an internet page open, click CTRL/APPLE + N) So the first step is to get the website page you want to link to up on the screen as well.

If you're already on the internet:
Get a new internet page up by clicking CTRL (OR APPLE KEY ON MAC) + N.

If you're writing in a document:
Open the internet page you want to hyperlink to.

Highlight the address in the target site address bar. And click CTRL + C (for copy).

Return to your document.

Highlight the word you want to hyperlink from.

Click INSERT from the toolbar that runs across the top of your computer screen.

Select HYPERLINK and a box will appear.

Place cursor in the LINK screen that runs across the top of the box and press CTRL + V (for pasting copy).

The website address will transfer to the box. Click OK.

A line will appear under the word.

If you are writing your document in Open Office it's exactly the same process.

CHAPTER 11

HOW TO HYPERLINK CHAPTER HEADINGS AND MAKE A KINDLE CLICKABLE TOC – TABLE OF CONTENTS

When you list your chapter headings at the beginning of your book, don't put corresponding page numbers. Instead you hyperlink the heading to the chapter concerned. This means the reader can click on any chapter heading and automatically be taken straight to that page.

Kindles also have a 'Click to Table Of Contents (TOC)' facility for readers as part of the actual hardware. If you embed the technical code instructions into your document, your reader can quickly navigate through your ebook at any time by pressing a button which will take them to the hyperlinked chapter listings at the front of your book. This is especially important for non-fiction reference books.

Inserting Clickable TOC – Table Of Contents
You can find the simplest set of instructions on how to embed a TOC in Kindle's June 2012 simplified guide *Building Your Book For Kindle*. Available free for both PC and Mac from the Amazon Kindle Store. I first tried to do the TOC thing with my PC Laptop, thinking that I would be covered for the tedious technical 'updates' that renders my old Mac useless on so many techie

update occasions. I got so far, but then came totally unstuck because I don't have the full, costly, version of Word on my PC Laptop, just the shortened version that the computer is sold with. GAH! So only embark on that route if you have more than the Starter Word kit installed on your PC. However, the Mac instructions tell you how to do it all manually, which works on a PC as well.

First, go through your text chapter by chapter, highlighting each chapter heading and labelling it HEADING 1. To find HEADING 1, look at your top horizontal toolbar. Modern versions of Word will have a HOME tab, which is where you'll find it. Older versions have a little window called TEXT BODY and you'll find it in the drop down menu.

So, you've been through your text labelling your chapter headings HEADING 1 (NOT 2,3,4 etc, just 1). The font will often change colour and position quite alarmingly. Don't worry, when you're done, just go through each one again changing it back to your preferred style, which won't delete the hidden link at all.

Next, type out your list of chapters at the front of your book, under the heading TABLE OF CONTENTS. Next, hyperlink each chapter number (see instructions below).

CHECK the hyperlinks are all working correctly.

Next, highlight the TABLE OF CONTENTS heading of your chapter list. Go to INSERT at the very top of your computer screen commands > BOOKMARK. A box will appear. Under the command BOOKMARK NAME, type three letters: toc. (no full stop) Click > ADD.

Hyperlinking

There is a wonderful video on You Tube that takes you through all the stages of turning your Open Office document into a PDF file. It also shows you how to make these hyperlinks and how to make your PDF document 'secure'. This is something you have to do before sending your book out to the public so that nobody can hack into it and change the content.

The You Tube video was made with no creator credited or I'd write his name loud and clear, it's here http://www.youtube.com/watch?v=Scp5ktP7j34 and called: Creating PDF Ebooks With Open Office.

I'll explain it step by step as best I can below but you'll grasp how to do it so much faster if you watch the clip.

How to make chapter hyperlinks in Open Office:

Click on FORMAT (running across top of your computer screen) > Styles & Formatting

A box opens with a list of Headings. First you have to assign a Heading number to each chapter. Go to the opening page of your first chapter. Position your cursor at the end of the first chapter title, CHAPTER ONE, and double click on Heading 1. This often turns the text into bold and sometimes a completely different font, even a different coloured font. Don't worry about that for the moment.

Put the cursor at the end of CHAPTER TWO chapter title and double click Heading 1 again for chapter 2. Etc.

When you've done this go back to your chapter list. Highlight Chapter 1 by holding your mouse over the beginning of 'Chapter' and moving it to the end of the chapter title and releasing the click.

Now you're ready to Hyperlink the chapter heading to the actual chapter.

Go to the commands right at the very top of your screen: INSERT > Hyperlink (or click the hyperlink symbol on your toolbar).

A little screen appears. First click the 'Document' icon on the left of this little screen, the one with the green arrow pointing down.

Then click the image of the target icon in the centre of the three choices, under 'Target'.

A new little window opens to the left of the screen.

Click on 'Headings' and then click on the relevant chapter listed. Be careful about double clicking here as you can cancel your action out. Before going on to the next stage make sure there's a broken line surrounding your chosen chapter.

Double click Apply in the smaller window. See the words transfer to the larger window.

Double click Apply in the larger window.

You won't know if you've been successful until you've transferred the document to PDF, but if the chapter heading is now underlined you've probably done it.

BEFORE YOU GO ANY FURTHER DO A TEST! Transferring the document to PDF takes seconds. It's well worth checking you've cracked it before going through the whole document.

TO TEST:

Click FILE at the top of the Open Office command screen.

Click on Export to PDF.

Open your PDF (find in your 'documents' folder with same title as your Open Office file) and see if it works.

NB: Exporting to PDF in this quick way is only for testing. When exporting to your final PDF document there are other boxes to check for security and to ensure the document's not over-sized.

MAKING CORRECTIONS

If any of your links haven't taken. Go to the words you want hyperlinked then repeat INSERT > Hyperlink > Document > Target > Headings Scroll down and see if your desired chapter is in the Headings list. If it is, highlight it with the broken lines and click > APPLY. Delete the broken words in your text and, with the cursor where you want the words to appear, type them instead in 'TEXT' > APPLY.

If your desired chapter isn't in the Headings list. Repeat the process from the beginning. Go to your chapter. FORMAT > Styles & Formatting > Double Click any Heading. If the texting indent changes, you won't be able to change it by hitting backspace or deleting the blank spaces. You have to go to the margin tags at the top of the page and readjust (sounds obvious but it took me ages before I twigged that one).

How to make chapter hyperlinks in Word:

Go to the opening page of your first chapter. Position your cursor at the end of the

first chapter title, CHAPTER ONE.

Click INSERT > Bookmark.

Write in Bookmark Name (C1) (has to be short or it won't work). Do this with all your chapter titles throughout your ebook.

Go to the beginning of the document where you want your chapter listing to appear. Highlight the words you want linked, I.e. 'Chapter One' .

Click INSERT > Hyperlink.

Highlight 'Document' in banner window.

In the 'Anchor' window type in your Bookmark Name (C1) > OK.

And your hyperlinked chapter heading will underline. Continue through.

Once you've set up your chapters for hyperlinking you can use the same Headings again and again every time you wish to refer to something in a different chapter.

CHAPTER 12

CHECK YOUR LINKS

If your ebook is non-fiction, you may well have included links to relevant sites on the internet. Before publishing, check all your links are working. As not all ereaders are linked to the internet, you may want to write out the www. link in brackets next to your hyperlink. Alternatively notify your reader at the beginning that you've listed all links, chronologically, chapter by chapter, at the end of your book.

If your ebook is a novel, you may want to put links somewhere at the beginning or end. These could be to your online sales site and/or to your own Twitter, Blog and Facebook pages. If you're working in Word, you can do this from your wip (work in progress). If you're writing your document on Open Office, open the link by holding down CONTROL and clicking on the link.

From a content perspective:
Are your links a reliable, trustworthy source of information? You can, of course, link to opinion pieces as well, but make sure you're not presenting opinion as fact.

From a technical perspective:
Are the links main page documents that are likely to stay put? Or do they have long sub-categories of numbers and letters in the web address? This points to the possibility that they are more

likely to be taken down at some stage in the future and your book will be linking to blank pages.

A Word About Linking from your Website

Make sure your links don't carry your reader away from your main document. After cutting and pasting your link address into the window, check the 'Open In New Window' box. The position of this varies, when linking from my website it's opposite the word 'Target' .

The HTML code for opening in a new window is: target='_blank'

It is placed at the end of the opening block of HTML ie: Click here for <a 'http://blackbird-digitalbooks.com/10-good-reasons-to-lie-about-your-age/' target='_blank'>more information</a> about my novel. <div class='separator' style='clear: both; text-align: left;' > Check that when the link is opened a folder tab opens at the top of your site. Then, when the link is closed the reader is returned to your original page. It's not wise to put too many links on your website, especially on the first page. You're inviting your hard-won reader who's just hit on your site to go back off into the internet hinterlands again. Make sure they can get back to you easily.

CHAPTER 13

USING PHOTOGRAPHS ONLINE AND INSERTING THEM INTO YOUR DOCUMENT

Low quality, low pixel-count images are BETTER for internet publishing than high quality images.

A high quality image (the more pixel dots the higher the quality) is disastrous for websites, PDF documents and email, as they'll add to the download time. Smashwords has a file upload limit of 5MB.

The exception to this rule is if you're using KindleGen to make your Kindle Master. There you can use the highest quality, colour (if relevant) images you have. Their size will automatically be reduced in the transfer system to the best reproduction available at the time.

The longer it takes for a website to load, the more likely your reader is to give up and go elsewhere and the lower down the Google ranking list it will be. If you have several photographs on a page, they're going to add up and make the download even slower.

However, if you're thinking of making and selling print-on-demand copies of your book, or if you want your book cover to feature in glossy magazine reviews, you will need a high quality image. If you're hiring a designer to make your cover, bear this in mind. It's easy to make a low resolution copy of a quality image.

I found the whole resizing of photographs a nightmare. It was my main trip-up point when I made my first ebook. Since then I've discovered an excellent, really easy-to-use, free photo editing and resizing site, see below.

Basically it comes down to this:

Computer storage capacity is measured in Bytes. There are Kilobytes, Megabytes and Gigabytes. Each byte is one base unit (the space it takes to store one letter of a word).

Photos are sized in KB and MB

KB = Kilobyte and is appx 1,000 bytes MB = Megabytes and is appx 1,000,000 bytes You'll also come across photo sizings described as: DPI = Dots Per Linear Inch (the more dots the higher quality the image) PPI = Pixels Per Linear Inch (pixel is another word for dot).

And as actual dimensions, eg 2342 x 2332 (very high quality, around 3MB), or 120 x 120 (low quality, the size of a thumbnail).

Ideal Photo Sizing:

• Images for Kindle INTERIOR pictures: Kindle request a 'JPEG of at least 600 x 800 pixels. Any less than 300 x 400 are likely to be rejected.' However, when you load your document to Kindle you'll find that, whatever size you make your pictures on your Word master, in conversion they'll blow up to full Kindle page size. This leaves no room for text. Not even for a heading. To fix this, right click the picture and select 'FORMAT PICTURE'. Select 'SIZE' from the horizontal menu running across the top.

Make the width about 4.90cm/1.92in the height will then come out at about 3.7cm/1.45in (this will vary slightly depending on the size of your Master). Click OK.

• Images for Smashwords interiors: *Images work best if you keep their dimensions small. If your current image runs the length of a 6 inch wide page, it may not display properly on the smaller screens of some ereading devices. Restrict images to widths of around 500 pixels or less.'* Smashwords Style Guide •

Images for website: ideal size between 50KB and 100KB. 70, 72 or 75DPI is the standard expression.

• Images for Adobe PDF documents: when you transfer your document to PDF, be sure to tick the Reduce Image resolution box at 75DPI. This means there will be 75 dots, or pixels, widthways and 75 dots lengthways.

• Internet Book cover: Amazon Kindle requests a width of at least 625 pixels and a length of at least 1000 pixels. The recommended size for cover art is 1563 x 2000. Save at 72dpi (more about all these terms later). The preferred height/width ratio is 1:6. Smashwords widths must be at least 1400 to qualify for their premium catalogue. A cover of 1600 x 2560 will give you a ratio of 1:6 which will cover (sorry) both Amazon and Smashwords.

• When transferring images from your own photo files, make sure they're not too big for the Web. I always follow the eBay suggested basic sizing when exporting rectangular stills from my photo files for the web, which is 1024 x 768.

If you are going to submit your cover to glossy print magazines, they require a size of 300DPI. The dpi is what enable print publications to publish good pics (the more dots per inch – the crisper/clearer the pic). The file size for a high quality image is between 1 and 5 Meg. Print picture editors have sometimes asked me for high quality below 2 Meg so that's a good average to go on.

There are picture editors already installed on computers called 'Paint' and 'Microsoft Picture Editor' and free Image Conversion sites like Gimp.

I use http://www.picmonkey.com/ which is good for making ebook covers and for simple picture resizing in a flash.

See also the excellent free online photo editing system http://pixlr.com/editor/ which is a little more advanced and less user-friendly than Picmonkey but has a wide PALLETE CHOICE for making ebook covers. Under 'BRUSH' selection click 'MORE' to see a massive selection of image and style options: Artistic, Nature, Shapes, Makeup, Misc. This gives the option of producing a cover entirely on this site without the need for any background art at all. PicMonkey's simplicity makes it my first choice for fast resizing of images for ebook covers and ebook picture inserts.

I have just been through the magazine process again with a popular women's magazine. The editor requested a photo of me 2 – 3 MG and an image of the book cover 1 – 2 MG. She didn't mention 300dpi. I suppose she took it as read. I did some more research and found this article by Rideau-info.com which questions the concept of 300dpi in the digital age. 'Photographic quality is a holdover from the quality of printing equipment a decade ago.' *What Print Shops Really Want:* http://www.rideau-info.com/photos/printshop.html. I wasn't sure if the magazine wanted 300dpi or if it's now a myth but did find some simple, clear instructions of how to make your image 'information' read 300dpi using photoshop. Which starts off: *'Possibly one of the most confusing aspects of dealing with digital imagery is resolution-specifically, what it really is and how changing it affects an image. You'd be shocked at the number of brilliant designers who don't know how to change an image from 72 dpi to 300 dpi-without turning it into a pile of pixel mush. That is, until now...'* Phew. So it's not just me then. Read this article on resizing to 300dpi, from Layers Magazine, the How-to-magazine-for-everything-Adobe:
http://layersmagazine.com/photoshop-resizing-images.html

Sending images over the Internet

Don't send large images over the internet. You'll clog up your sendee's in box and not only look unprofessional but could lose a client/friend/customer forever. I know because I did it. Luckily the recipient was a very understanding friend. The maximum size for sending as an attachment is usually 1 or 2 Meg, but some internet connections struggle with 1 Meg, especially if you're sending more than 1 image. Check the lettering at the end of your image, if it's KB you're fine. Beware especially of TIFFs. They have excellent image quality but are way too big and need to be reduced before sending. If you have a large image or file, send it via the free backup and online file sharing site DropBox or, if emailing is the only way (to a busy picture editor for example), send large images one at a time.

HOW TO ADD PHOTOS INTO YOUR DOCUMENT

There are, I'm sure, several ways you can do this but this was my way which is fairly straightforward. Update suggestions welcome.

So, you're writing away, blah de blah blah blah, and you have an image you've taken with your camera or iPhone that you want to include in your ebook. You put the photo in to your master Word or Open Office document by clicking INSERT > Picture and then selecting the image from your document list.

Step by Step:

• Transfer the shot from your camera to your computer.

• Before exporting to your desktop, see if you can make the image any better by using the editing tools. Some handy, simple one-click ones to try: 'Crop' can you take out any unnecessary space around the edge of the image? Keep everything balanced though.

'Enhance' enriches the image by enhancing the contrast between colours.

'Effects' + 'Boost Colour' deepens the colours.

'Adjust' +'Straighten' extremely handy tool for images that don't have horizontal horizons. Never, ever publish a photograph with horizons that aren't straight unless it's for artistic effect. Which most book illustrations aren't.

• When you're happy with your image. Click FILE > Export •
A box comes up with your export options: FORMAT > JPG.

• Under SIZE select 1024 x 768, or if it's not landscape (horizontal image) but a portrait (upright image) select 768 x 1024 (don't worry about this, the computer will only let you do it the correct way). If your image is square select 1024 x 1024, again, if it's not quite square the computer will automatically insert the actual ratio.

• Select a name for your picture and click EXPORT.

• Close all windows (or hit F11 on a Mac) and find your image on your desktop (if no name given it'll be 'Picture 1').

• Click on the name box and type in a title (for me, this is ROBIN) followed by a dot and write jpg (Robin.jpg). This is very important. The computer will throw a box up saying 'Are You Sure?' and you click 'Add' . Without the dot and the jpg the image will be rejected when you try to import it.

• Now go back to your document. Select INSERT from the list of commands at the very top of your computer screen > PICTURE > From File. Your computer files will come up.

Click DESKTOP and search for your photograph title. Click it and the image will appear.

• You can now resize the image by clicking on it and dragging the little square boxes.

• You can move the image down, up, to the right, to the left by clicking inside the image and dragging your mouse.

• Look critically at your image one more time now it's on the page. Can it be improved? If so go through the process again.

ANCHORING

Click on the anchor symbol to anchor the image to the page and stop it moving around. Then if you make any changes to an earlier part of the document your page layout won't be thrown into chaos. If there's no anchor visible:

Open Office:
Right click the image > Anchor > To Page
Word:
Right click the image > Format Picture > Layout > Advanced > Lock Anchor • OR
Layout > Advanced
Then 2 options at the top Picture Position/Text Wrapping. If you click on Picture Position you get the Lock Anchor option.

• OR

Format > position > more layout options > click Lock Anchor Depending on the year of your Word Software.

HOW TO CHECK YOUR PHOTO IMAGE SIZE

Right click your mouse on the image and click 'Properties'. Or go to TOOLS > Get Info.

HOW TO CHANGE YOUR PHOTO IMAGE FROM JPG TO GIF

GIF stands for Graphics Interchange Format. The downside of GIF is that it supports far fewer colours than JPG, something like 250 as against 16 million. It's great for blocks of colour and text, though, so some ebook covers will come out better in GIF. Something to experiment with. GIF reproduces sharper line-art and text and is the format Amazon advises for photo insert images of text or tables in Kindle. To change your JPG image to GIF, put the image up on your screen:

FILE > Save As > Select GIF format.

If you've manually labelled the image to (eg) robin.jpg in the exporting process then change the label to robin.gif.

WHAT'S PNG?

PNG is another image option you'll see offered. The images are of very high quality but my standard robin photo came out at 3168 x 2539 and a massive 9.5MB (but, still at 72dpi, no good for publication). So it's unsuitable for sending out as ebooks, email or for using on web pages. Useful if you want to print high quality images. Smashwords also accept PNG images for their thumbnail book covers.

HOW TO TAKE A SCREENSHOT

On a Mac, hold your mouse over the top left corner of the image, hold down CTRL/APPLE + SHIFT + 4 on your keyboard. The little hand cursor turns into a circle with a cross through it. Drag your mouse across the image and release the keys when your image is fully shaded. You'll hear a shutter click. The thumbnail will now be on your desktop, labelled Picture 1. Retitle it and add a dot and the letters jpg at the end. Without this dot and jpg you won't be able to transfer your image to the web.

PCs have various methods depending on the model. Most now have a PRNT.SCR key on the keyboard. Press this and you'll get a shot of the whole screen. To screenshot the image only, the procedure is to open your Word document and then press ALT at the same time as PRNT.SCR. Later PCs have a SNIPPING TOOL.

WHAT IF YOUR PHOTOS SUDDENLY ALL DISAPPEAR FROM YOUR OPEN OFFICE DOCUMENT?

As happened to me, causing major panic.

If all the graphics suddenly disappear and you're left with a blank space with a number in the corner where there should be colour images this is what you do. (So simple and basic when you know how but this took me about half a day to solve): VIEW > Toolbars > Tools

A little box with various symbols will appear.

Graphics on/off is 2nd in from the right.

Click this and all your pictures will reappear.

HOW TO CAPTION PHOTOS FOR KINDLE

The problem with captioning photos is that the text and the images are not linked. The solution was found for me by Mark Binner, the author of the extra techie chapter at the end of this book.

'Because Kindle users can change the font size of text, you cannot guarantee that a photo caption, for example, will remain on the same 'page' as the photo it refers to. The result can look rather untidy. One solution is to edit the photo with a photo editor and put the caption inside the photo. Then the caption becomes part of an image rather than text.'

Go to PicMonkey (free) and add an OVERLAY > Select the 'speech bubble' symbol on the Main Menu to the far L > Select the top 'Geometric' option > Select the rectangle and add it to your image > when you have sized and positioned this and chosen the correct b/g colour (normally white for a caption), add your caption text on top. You might find it a bit less fiddly to save the image without the text first, then you can fiddle with your caption text without the background shifting about.

COPYRIGHT

In case you've turned to this page without reading the whole book, the info below is repeated from the copyright chapter:

For free stock photos go to http://compfight.com/ For free graphics go to http://www.freevector.com/.

There you will find a huge selection of images. Some are free for private use only, others for private and commercial use. There is a special page for commercial use: http://qvectors.net/tag/commercial-use/page/2/.

ALWAYS credit and link, if possible, to the source.

CHAPTER 14

HOW TO MAKE OR COMMISSION AN EBOOK COVER

You *can,* of course, tell a lot about a book by its cover. I admit I have made some spectacular mistakes in the past when money was… well, there simply was no money when I started out. If you have any money to invest in your project, hiring a professional designer to make your cover is a good place to put it. Fena Lee (http://pheeena.carbonmade.com/) is a design student living in Singapore. Fena designs great covers for $100/£62 with any subsequent designs at $75. For this you get up to 3 different high res covers plus unlimited editing. If you have money to invest, at the very top end, Nuno Moreira at http://www.bookcovers-design.com is my #1 favourite, he's great to work with and has truly inspired vision.

At the budget end, Jes Richardson at http://www.coverbistro.com is another really good person to work with. She kindly got me through an Ingram/Spark cover formatting glitch. Jes offers one-off pre-made covers as well as bespoke design. These covers are designed to fit certain genres, you pick your cover and it's taken off the sales website and not offered for sale to any other author. It's not something I have tried.

I also like the look of The Cover Collection. For £30 ($50) you get 'a unique ebook cover using top quality photographic images (price includes licensed permissions up to 250,000 copies), addition of your own book title, your author name and any tag line or quotes you would like to appear on your cover. You will receive multiple drafts to choose from (approx. 7-10) and unlimited revisions until you are 100% happy.' Visit this link to browse their current offerings: http://www.thecovercollection.com/premade-ebook-kindle-covers/prices/ Or you could place an ad in, or look at www.peopleperhour.com (UK), www.elance.com (US) or www.fiverr.com.

If you think you might want to make a paperback some time in the future, the standard size known as American Trade, used most commonly at the free paperback-building site CreateSpace and at IngramSpark is 6in x 9in. As I said earlier, I prefer 5.5in x 8.5in. If you ask for either size at 300dpi this can easily be sized down to 72dpi for Kindle, Draft2Digital and Smashwords.

Read about the latest thoughts on ebook design (Square covers? Covers with no writing at all? Designing your cover with an iPhone App?) at Password Incorrect's excellent series ebook cover design series: http://www.passwordincorrect.com/tag/ebook-specific-cover-design/ The simplest way to make an ebook cover is with a still photo plus text. Or you could use a piece of artwork instead of the photograph (if the artwork's not yours, get written permission to use the work, even if it's by a friend or relative).

Photoshop (costs but free trial available) and Gimp (free but techy) are the advanced options that need some studying to find your way around. There are lots of online tutorials at YouTube to assist. I have mastered Gimp now, and find its advanced features really useful, namely the choice, and crispness, of fonts. There are lots of free fonts that can be transferred to Gimp from online free resources, my favourite being http://www.fontsquirrel.com/

Gimp isn't for techie beginners though and, in case you didn't come here from the last chapter, I'll say it again: for beginners, http://www.picmonkey.com is a fantastic, free, simple to use, photo editing site for making ebook covers and resizing images. See also the excellent free online photo editing system Pixlr.

One of the reasons I used to make my own covers more often than using a designer for my own books was that, apart from really serious, not-funny, financial restraints, I liked to experiment with titles on Kindle. If I paid for a cover to be designed I felt more restricted.

Book cover design is of course an art unto itself. Keeping things simple and clear is likely to produce the best results in your own, non-professional hands: • First do what the mainstream publishers' designers do and look at the books in your genre in the Amazon charts. Look for obvious style similarities in image, colour and font. Being Different and Original isn't going to help get your book noticed any unless you're a design genius.

• Are the words large and clear? Is centred text bang in the middle? (use a ruler or tape measure on the screen) • Do the words clash with the image? • Make sure the words are bold and readable and that no colours bleed into the background.

• Don't be too cavalier with font mixing (2 max for beginners).

Study the whole fascinating world of fonts and typography at Joel Friedlander's http://www.thebookdesigner.com/. Check out also his monthly ebook cover awards:
http://www.thebookdesigner.com/2012/12/e-book-cover-design-awards-november-2012/ for a host of visual tips on do's and don'ts.

CHAPTER 15

MAKING A DO IT YOURSELF COVER – FIND AFFORDABLE ARTWORK AND FREE ROYALTY-FREE PHOTOGRAPHS

To have any chance of sales success your ebook cover has got to stand up next to the professional designs. If you're not a designer it most likely won't. If you want to give it a go, don't be too ambitious. Aim for simple clarity.

How not to do it:

Go over to Amazon Kindle ebookstore and type one of the craft hobbies or 'gardening' into the search window. Scroll down the images and pick out the home-made covers. Easy to spot?

Using Your Own Photograph/Artwork

I've a lot to learn about graphics and colour but I've had quite a few photographs published in books and magazines and have a reasonably good camera. Before I found my cover designer, I chose to make my book cover using one of my own stills.

If you're an artist or have one in the family you could of course use your own artwork instead of a photograph. Don't take any images from the web that you haven't got permission to use.

Using Professional Photographs

If you're not confident, the best compromise is to buy a professionally-shot image from an online photo agency and then put your own title graphics over the top. If you mess up on the graphics it doesn't matter. At least you've tried. You can keep the image and hire a graphic artist to put the title words up for you. Costs vary but a designer shouldn't cost more than about £40/$60. If you've invested a lot of time and effort into writing your book, this will be money well spent.

You can buy a royalty-free photo very cheaply online. Look at good stock photo agencies like Shutterstock and istockphoto. Join for free and search the enormous files of images. Type in your subject or abstract expressions that suit your story like 'fear' or 'terror' or 'love' and see what comes up. I find myself using Dreamstime, http://dreamstime.com more than any other site. They have free images and many that cost just a few dollars. See also stock.xchng which advertises itself as the leading free stock photo site, and BigStockPhoto which is more than affordable. As mentioned in the Copyright chapter: For free stock photos go to http://compfight.com/ For free graphics go to http://qvectors.net/tag/commercial-use/page/2/.

ALWAYS credit and link, if possible, to the source.

Photograph Sizes

Stills at istockphoto come in sizes: xsmall, small, medium, large, xlarge, xxlarge. **Remember, for the internet you don't need a high quality photo!** A size that will work for both Kindle and Smashwords book covers is 1600 x 2560 at 72dpi. If making a print book cover, go for the smallest 300dpi image and resize for Kindle/Smashwords at Picmonkey. Costs vary depending on which image you choose, but one of my favourite images would cost about $8.

Using Professional Artwork

Craftspeople and artists from all over the world use http://www.etsy.com to sell their work direct to the customer.

If you fancy having an original piece of art on your cover, have a look at the Art section. Remember you're looking for a portrait image (long/tall/book-shaped) rather than landscape (wide/horizontal).

• Check the box: Sort by > Most relevant.

• Try putting a word into the Search box that relates to the content of your book . It could be concrete (house, tree, china) or abstract (fear, hate, love).

Saatchi Online is a free display and sales resource for artists, art students, photographers, illustrators and video artists.

Deviant Art with over 100 million original works of art, is another major platform for artists and designers.

If you find a work of art you like, you may be able to do a deal. You don't, after all, need to own the actual image though some are affordable (they start from just a few pounds/dollars).

Sell your ebook to the artist as a platform for their work, with a credit and link to their website displayed inside, and you might get it for nothing. You will be driving customers to the artist and perhaps the artist will return the favour, putting your book, with their lovely cover, up on their site.

If you are buying an image to use on your cover, tell the artist what you're doing. They'll probably be delighted but you'll need their written permission for commercial use before you close the deal.

The popularity of Tumblr is racing. Search under the #art hashtag.

When you make your first enquiries, make it clear you're only at the research stage of your quest for your perfect book cover and that there are several contenders you're thinking about. Even if you're pretty sure you've found exactly what you want, creative decisions aren't fixed in stone. It could be the next time you visit the site you'll find an image you love even more. When you think you've found what you want, let the decision simmer for a few days. Don't make any final offer until you're sure you've found the image you want to use.

CHAPTER 16

HOW TO MAKE A THUMBNAIL COVER

This is the little picture of the cover of your book you put on all the sales sites.

Go to Picmonkey, upload your image and resize at 1600 x 2560, suitable for Amazon, Draft2Digital and Smashwords. Also make a smaller image with a 400 pixel width for use on the Web, for your website, to insert into blog items etc. Also make another tiny image at 73 x 100 or thereabouts for your Twitter Avatar (picture profile).

Makeathumbnail.com and Fookes are two free thumbnail download sites.

If, for some reason, you don't have the internet, or your picture fails to load, this is how to do it on your computer (and the way I did it, not knowing about the above at the time).

For MAC: Press CTRL + SHIFT + 4.

Your mouse cursor image changes to a circle with a cross symbol through it.

For PC: Select the SNIPPING TOOL which works in a similar way. (If you can't see it put 'snipping' in FIND on main menu.) Hold this circle with cross symbol over the top left corner of your image and drag your mouse down to the bottom right of the image. Let go of Command/shift/4 and (on a Mac) you'll hear a click. The image will now be on your desktop.

If your desktop is crowded, to find this image quickly, minimise all files that are open and click anywhere on the home screen to bring up your desktop command column that runs across the top of the screen starting with FINDER (it continues: File Edit View etc).

Click on VIEW > Arrange By > DATE MODIFIED or DATE CREATED.

Your thumbnail will now be at the top right of your screen. Let's say it's called Cat.

Before you can download this image, it needs to have a dot in the title plus jpg at the end. To do this: Click on the icon once.

Then click on the CAT lettering once. This will highlight a box that surrounds the lettering.

You can now re-type your picture title. Double click on the letters CAT below the icon. Retype the word Cat, but add the dot and jpg. So it'll now be Cat.jpg

Your thumbnail is now a .jpg file and ready to import onto the web.

CHAPTER 17

DIFFERENT PHOTO SIZING FOR COVERS, DOCS AND PUBLICITY

In Chapter 13 I attempted to guide you through the maze of photo sizing descriptions.

Basically it boils down to this: **WEB** 72dpi **PRINT** 300dpi Images for magazines, posters and print book covers need to be made in a much higher resolution (dpi – dots per inch, pixel ratio) than images for the web. Images for the web, on the other hand, need to be of a low resolution. Low quality images won't reproduce in print, high quality images take too long to download on the web and can clog up email systems if you attempt to send as attachments. If you are making an Adobe PDF ebook, make sure you lower the image resolution (see Chapter 19).

As it's not a problem to resize an image from high to low resolution, when you are thinking about your master image for your book cover consider its future. Are you planning to print copies of your book as well as selling over the web? Are you going to try and get your book reviewed in newspapers and magazines? Will you want to print flyers or posters? If so, make your cover using a high quality image and reduce it for the web (see Chapter 13). To have a cover design ready-made for standard US Trade Paperback, good for the free Lulu and CreateSpace paperback cover creators, and that will also function as an ebook cover, ask your graphic designer for: 5.5in x 8.5in at 300dpi.

All text must be at least 0.5in from the outer edges.

CHAPTER 18

FINAL TOUCHES

Non-Fiction: Reviewing Your Target Market

If you're writing in a country outside the USA you'll probably want to make your book as US-friendly as possible.

If your book is non-fiction, read through your document as an American. If it includes shopping advice, check that all prices are given a US dollar equivalent in brackets.

Give the exchange rate you used at the beginning of the book. If there's a major currency shift in the news, consider updating your prices and republishing.

Make sure any measurements given in kilometres, litres and kilograms have the alternative US-friendly miles, pounds and ounces.

Fiction: Last Minute Worries

A fiction book is of its own world and regional details shouldn't be tampered with.

The problem is, when do you stop tampering with your writing style and the story itself? Even when I'm convinced I've finished, every time I do another read-through I find more that needs fiddling with. Many authors find there comes a point where they just have to 'let go' of their work before they feel it's quite ready.

If you're a published author with a deadline for your next novel, time running out often makes the decision for you. At least you know you'll have your agent's feedback, and then your editor's, to come.

If you're self-published, you may, if you're lucky, have friends and relatives who'll read your novel and tell you what they think of it. But there's always that niggling feeling – how honest are they being? Taking criticism may be hard, but giving it is a minefield.

It's difficult to get the balance of a writing group right. I belonged to one for about 10 years. We critiqued each others' work once a fortnight and shared our many excitements and disappointments along the way. Our critique method grew out of a creative writing adult education class, where the core members of the group first met. The classes are still going – in Richmond, west of London. I started at the beginner's class and, after 2 years, moved on to the advanced workshop. After my novels were published, I returned to the college as a guest tutor several times and helped judge their annual short story competition.

Our group ran on similar lines to the advanced class: read and respond. The only rule was that nobody read for longer than 10 minutes.

Final Words

Do you want to add a links page at the end of your book?

Acknowledgements?

Have you any other books published you want to mention? Any forthcoming books you want to mention? Links to your Twitter, Facebook website pages where readers can leave feedback? Are there any links to contributors' websites you could include? The tradition of link-swapping in ebooks is a healthy inheritance from the free spirit of the online blogging community. Only include links when they're really relevant to the content. I've recommended 2 friends and colleagues in this book, I've known them for years and worked with both of them.

CHAPTER 19

PUBLISHING TO ADOBE PDF

Only for PDF originals. PDFs are not suitable for uploading to content ebook sales sites.

OK Your MS is ready to be turned into an ebook:

Click FILE.

Click EXPORT TO PDF.

Keep jpeg compression at 99% but tick REDUCE IMAGE RESOLUTION box and reduce to 75DPI (THIS IS VITAL AND ISN'T IN THE YOU TUBE GUIDE) When you make your final MASTER COPY of your ebook you will want to make it secure by clicking SECURITY at the very top of the transfer box. But ignore that for now. You need to see, by trial and error, how it's all going to look. There'll be several transfers needed to get the placing of your chapters and images exactly right.

Now if you go to your document file you'll see the PDF ready to open.

Open your Master Open Office (or Word) document and put it up on the screen next to your Adobe PDF transfer. Make your corrections on this MS, not the Adobe PDF which you can't write on. When your corrections are done, retransfer to a new PDF.

CHECKLIST

Check that the spacing is correct and consistent. Are your stills in exactly the right place? Is the text wrapping around stills as you want it? If not, right click on the image, select Wrap and the image you desire I.e do you want the words to appear on the left of the picture, on the right of the picture, or do you want the picture to be centred in isolation without the words of the text running on below it? When you're fiddling with the spacing of the whole document, you might find the beginning of chapters and the chapter headings move about a bit. Every time before you transfer to PDF from your Master Word or Open Office Document, scroll through to make sure each chapter starts on a new page and the heading is approximately a third of the way down the page.

This is important because when you make small changes as you fiddle with the positioning, it gives you leeway to add a sentence here and there without the alignment of the whole book getting out of sync.

If you add a line to a chapter, try and keep a note of how many extra lines you've included. Then go back to the beginning of the chapter and move the chapter heading up by the same number of lines. This will return the spacings for the chapters in the rest of the book back to how they were before you made your correction. If you already have an earlier Adobe transfer you can match the following page of your new draft to the original. By matching the final lines of the following page you will have realigned the whole book from thereon.

When you've completed a read-through and made corrections, save your Master MS with a number, 2CatMaster, 3CatMaster etc. Then, when you transfer again to PDF it will be easy to identify the latest version. If you don't do this numbering system you could lose track of which document is your final document and get in a mess.

When you're happy with how the PDF looks:
Do a final proofread from the final PDF document (See next chapter).

Check the words again with particular attention to the spaces and where the pages start and finish.

Check the links are all working.

If this isn't a book PDF but an ebook PDF, do a final double-check that you've reduced the resolution image to 75DPI.

When you make your final MASTER COPY of your ebook you will want to make it secure by clicking SECURITY at the very top of the transfer box. See Chapter 21.

CHAPTER 20

FINAL PROOFREAD

When all your words and artwork are in place, the next step is to do a final proofread. This is where you look very closely at each word and each space between the words to check that all the commas, full stops, hyphens, apostrophes etc are in the right place. Are all the spacings even and symmetrical? If you're not up to scratch on spelling and grammar this is the one area, apart from cover design, where you might want to think about getting professional help. This is because proofreading creates the biggest chasm between amateur and professional presentation. Think of all the hours and days spent writing your book – it would be a real shame to let it fall at this post.

Even when a book has been read by a series of professional editors and their experienced in-house readers it's astonishing what mistakes can get through.

Don't hit the 'publish' button until you're confident of your content and presentation. If hiring a professional proofreader is out of the question, badger friends and contacts until you find somebody with the skills you need.

With any luck there won't be more than one or two slip-ups and your reputation will stay intact. Any more than this, or one glaring error near the beginning, and you risk your reader doing the book equivalent of throwing your book down in disgust – hitting delete. Not bothering to read on to the end of the first 3 free sample chapters. Not bothering to pay for the rest of your content.

You haven't taken care to present your work to them properly, so why should they go on believing what they're reading? You're entering a fragile contract of trust with your reader. Early mistakes will not be tolerated – subconsciously, if not consciously. Regarding costs, Sarah Tomley of Editors Online: http://www.editorsonline.org/Publisher_Services.html says you should expect to pay around £8/$11 per 1,000 words for fiction and £10 /$14 per 1,000 words for non-fiction. With non-fiction her company is checking so much more (all the essential topics are covered, and ordered in logical chapters, all the pictures and captions are there and correct, all the names and facts are correct and so on), so it takes longer. Sarah was my non-fiction editor at Hamlyn and is the only editor I can personally recommend.

If you're doing it yourself, look for all the tiny details like spelling and typos. Are there commas where there should be full stops? Are all the apostrophes in the right place? It's easy to get carried away with exclamation marks when you're writing. Delete them! Except where they're really necessary!! Otherwise you'll startle your reader!! Are your quotes consistent. 'Curly quotes' are the standard for fiction speech. If you use single quotes for speech, use "double quotes" for quoting anything else within the text. Or vice versa.

Have you got any ragged margins? Ie is all your text justified to the right so that there's a clean line down the right hand side of the page? Calibre default is not set at justification and may need adjusting. Instructions in next chapter. The full stop goes WITHIN the quote for speech, OUTSIDE the quote for 'quoting'.

Are the spaces between sentences correct? A common mistake is to leave two spaces after the end of every full stop which is correct for letters and other documents. In publishing it's one gap.

Here's the BBC's guide to common mistakes in proofreading: http://www.bbc.co.uk/skillswise/english Oh, and for Adobe PDF, ie non toilet-roll presentation, are there hanging, single lines at the end of chapters? If so, try moving the chapter heading up a space, shortening a sentence to get you an extra line or combining a paragraph somewhere.

Using Your Kindle As An Editing Tool For writers and editors there's an extra incentive to get Kindled-up, and that's the editing tool. Be it a book, a dissertation, a company report, you can email your own work to your Kindle with the special email you're given with your purchase. Or you can transfer it direct from your computer. Your MS magically transforms into 'book'. A nice chunk of that all-important distance is added that doesn't happen when you read to edit from the screen, or even from paper. You can highlight text and add in notes as you read. When you're ready to go back to your next computer edit you can bring your edits up as a list.

To transfer a MS to Kindle via your computer, email it to yourself via your special kindle email.

This will be your Amazon account sign in email eg: s.bloggs@blueyonder.com with the alteration: s.bloggs@free.kindle.com

More complicated, but possible, is to do it via the free ebook management system Calibre.

Save your file as a HTML.

Import it into Calibre via the 'Add Books To Calibre Library' Red book icon top L.

Plug your Kindle into your computer with the charger lead which adapts for this purpose.

Highlight the title in Calibre.

Click the Blue 'Send To Device' icon in the centre of the top toolbar. Voila. Calibre will detect the type of e-reader and transfer the appropriate ebook system automatically.

To edit on your kindle click on that big, square button at any point in the text and start writing, a window will open up at the bottom of your Kindle screen. Click 'save' in this window and continue reading until your next edit.

To view your notes click MENU, then 'View Notes And Marks'.

CHAPTER 21

HOW TO SET UP SECURITY ON ADOBE PDF

For a step by step visual guide, scroll through to 6'45 on this You Tube video Creating PDF ebooks with Open Office:

http://www.youtube.com/watch?v=Scp5ktP7j34

Transferring your Open Office or Word file to PDF: Click FILE > Export as PDF.

Keep jpeg compression at 99% but tick REDUCE IMAGE RESOLUTION box and reduce to 75DPI (THIS IS VITAL AND ISN'T IN THE YOU TUBE GUIDE) To make your file secure, click SECURITY (right at the top of the PDF box) > Set Permission Password.

Enter in a password.

Click GENERAL to go back to original screen.

Click EXPORT.

CHAPTER 22

CONVERTING TO KINDLE MOBI & EPUB ON CALIBRE AND LOADING YOUR EBOOKS TO AMAZON KDP AND KOBO SALES SITES

How To Convert to Mobi and Epub On CalibreNow to Calibre:

http://calibre-ebook.com/.

As stated earlier, if you're using an older version of Calibre on an old Mac it won't probably work. You'll have to beg or borrow a PC or modern Mac that will download the latest version of Calibre which is a breeze, formatting-wise, compared to the older versions. Watch the simple tutorial video which shows you what all the basic buttons do.

First make a new file on your desktop to store Calibre ebooks. Open the list of computer files and folders at your computer START or Apple button. The list will be something like ComputerUser'sName/Documents/Music/Games/Computer/Control Panel. You need to click the Computer User's Name, which will probably be your login name at the top of the list. Then go to > New Folder and label it CALIBRE. You will now have a Calibre Folder on your desktop.

Open the Calibre Dashboard. Click 'ADD BOOKS' top Left. > Look for your ComputerUsersName label > from there you can get to your documents. Select your HTML file.

It will be added to your Calibre library.

Next to ADD BOOKS is a blue EDIT METADATA icon. Select 'Edit Metadata'.

Check title and author are filled in correctly. If your ebook is already online, go to bottom and click 'Download Metadata' and Calibre will automatically fill in description, cover etc.

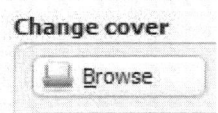

If the ebook and/or cover is new, click 'Browse' (Just underneath 'Change Cover' heading) to find your cover to add.

Now you're almost ready to convert your text into an ebook. An important doublecheck is to ensure that the margins are justified to the right, ie that they are in 'book' format where the text is all boxed to the right just as it is to the left, rather than running 'ragged' to the right as it would in normal typed text.

At Top R of the Screen is a PREFERENCES icon – a set of b/w cogs and wheels . CLICK.

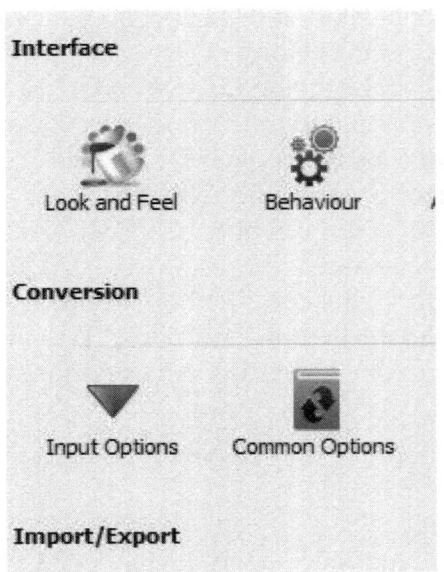

Under Conversion, 2nd row down, is COMMON OPTIONS a brown book icon. CLICK.

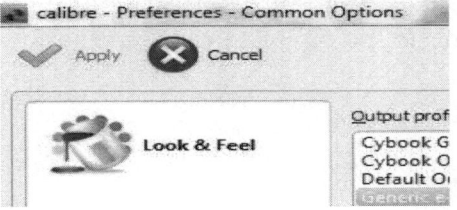

Now look Top L for a LOOK & FEEL coloured paintpot icon. CLICK.

Text Justification options are at the bottom of this page.

A window on the R of the page might say LEFT ALIGN. Open this window and select JUSTIFY TEXT. Then click the GREEN APPLY TICK top left to set this command.

Now click the brown 'convert books' icon at the top next to Metadata icon.

A window will open. TOP RIGHT of this window is a drop-down box with the various ebook formats. Select MOBI (or EPUB) and CLICK.

A wheel will spin on the bottom right. When this has stopped. You'll see, on the right just below the cover image, that MOBI (OR EPUB) has been added to the formats.

Right click on MOBI (OR EPUB) and a window 'Save The Mobi Format To Disk' will drop down. CLICK.

A window will open called 'Choose Destination Directory.' Just click 'SELECT FOLDER' button bottom R and your newly-created Mobi or Epub will transfer to your Desktop Calibre folder. Open it and check you're happy with the spacings etc. If you need to correct anything, delete the book file from the Calibre list and start again, correcting the Word document, converting to HTML, loading the HTML to Calibre, entering the cover and metadata, then click 'convert'.

Two possible spacing problems

There are two Calibre glitches that you may encounter at this stage which have nothing to do with errors in your Master document:

1) You may find that spaces, which weren't in your Master document, have appeared between each paragraph.

2) You may find that the first line of each chapter, which, to conform to the publishing norm, should start as a block paragraph flush to the L margin, has turned into an indented paragraph.

To correct these in Calibre:

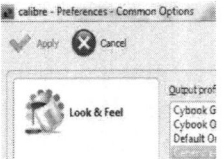

After you have your book loaded to Calibre and you have clicked CONVERT BOOK. Go to the LOOK AND FEEL paintpot on the top L again.

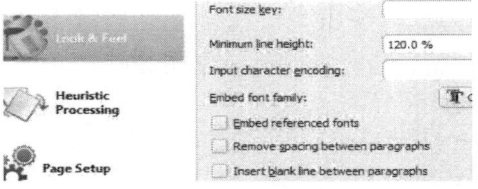

Then check that the REMOVE SPACING BETWEEN PARAGRAPHS window ISN'T ticked. Because if this is ticked it over-rides all other techie instructions and you won't get your block, no-indent, first paragraphs.

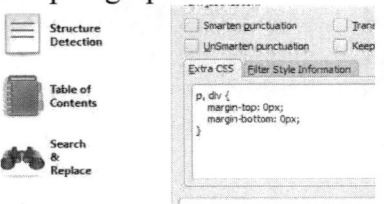

If you want to edit your Table of Contents, transfer first to EPUB, which has a TOC editing facility (click the TOC parallel lines icon below the 'Look And Feel' icon). You can also edit your text in ePub as well. Then load the EPUB to Calibre and transfer THAT to .mobi for Kindle.

And that's it. You have an ebook ready to load to the sales sites.

You are now done with Calibre.

Don't forget the 'Donate' heart if you can afford to give the Calibre people anything for providing this service free of charge.

Loading ePub to Kobo

Now go to Kobo Writing Life

http://www.kobobooks.com/kobowritinglife.

Scroll down to bottom of page and click START PUBLISHING.

The interface is very simple to follow. Fill in the title, author details and book description.

When you're prompted to upload your ePub book, you might see that Calibre has exported 3 files to the folder on your desktop. Select the top 'ePub' file, not the jpeg image or the OPF File (idents are on the far right of the line).

When it has uploaded you're invited to preview your Kobo ebook.

Look through – checking especially for spacings and that the chapter listings on the left hand side have come out OK.

If you're happy with the content, continue. If not, delete the file from Calibre, re-edit your master, retransfer to HTML and load to Calibre again.

Next you're asked to apply Digital Rights Management, which is set to default at YES. And then Geographic Rights, default set to yes.

As per my Kindle query on this where I was advised not to apply DRM, I choose not to do this and select NO. As I hold world rights on my title I keep the YES there.

Set the price and hit PUBLISH.

Don't forget to fill out your account details so that royalties can be paid directly into your bank account every month.

If you have books with reviews on Goodreads, you can transfer those over to the Kobo site by adding the Kobo version with its unique ISBN (It's tiny – find it at the bottom right of the sales page) to Goodreads. Go to your book page at Goodreads and click 'edit details' to add the Kobo version ISBN.

A good blog to follow for all the latest Kindle information is Andrys Basten's http://kindleworld.blogspot.co.uk/.

For those not so familiar with computer-speak, there is also a Quickstart ABC Guide for total beginners in the Appendix of this ebook. This was created in response to an email from reader Alan Grainger (age 83) who found it all a bit too technical. He has now successfully ePublished all 8 of his books on Kindle and Smashwords Premium.

Having followed the layout guidelines in *Part Two – Turning Your Words Into An Ebook* your document will be almost ready to transfer onto Amazon's Digital Text Platform for Kindle.

Final Checks

Hit the backward P in the Word Toolbar (In Open Office: View > Nonprinting Characters) to bring up the hidden formatting markings: Check there are insert page breaks between chapters. (Place cursor at the end of the chapter, Click INSERT > Page Break.) Spacing is the main problem with this transfer process. Narrow down any wide gaps in spaces between the lines and even out any small gaps so that the same number of 'space' markings appear before and after. Even out Chapter Headings so that they are all starting at the same place on the page. Some small spacings may well appear much wider when you get to the final online check and will need closing up.

Loading to Amazon Digital

First, if you have any problems, Amazon digital email help:kdp-support@amazon.com are helpful and usually quick to respond.

Go to Amazon's Digital Text Platform.

Https://kdp.amazon.com/self-publishing/signin If you don't have a reader account with Amazon, create one.

SIGN IN

Click GETTING STARTED & FAQs.

View Amazon's How To Publish – Video Tutorial
https://kdp.amazon.com/self-publishing/help?
topicId=A2M7MM0UP7PHK0

Under the GETTING STARTED GUIDE > Publish Your ContentScroll down to START HERE TO PUBLISH YOUR CONTENT > Enter Your Product Details And you arrive at the first page of your dashboard.

Bookmark it.

1.Enter Details

The dashboard is your control panel where you'll enter:• Your sales blurb.

• Your thumbnail cover.

• The price you want to charge.

• The 7 keywords or phrases you'll want to use to help browsers find your book (think carefully and put in the most relevant and specific words or phrases you can come up with).

•The categories you want your book to appear under (eg fiction, healthy living, architecture, art, education). You can select up to 2 categories. To maximise your exposure, spend some time finding the two most relevant categories with the smallest amount of competition. For example, Romance is a very large category (135,239 in UK alone), whereas Family Saga has 5,035 books listed.

• Whether you want to enable DRM, Digital Rights Management, or not.

I found it all self-explanatory apart from DRM. Assuming more control would be better I ticked yes, enable please. But then read that buyers prefer DRM not to be there and it might hinder my sales. So I popped my Forum Cherry: Should I unpublish and start again, because once it's in you can't change it? The price, the description, even the book is easy to change and re-load but you can't change the DRM decision once made.

Here are the responses:

The vast majority of people won't be bothered by the DRM on the Kindle version.

That's good to know. They must encode it in such a way that they aren't comfortable stripping it out (or they don't want one version with it and one without it running around because it may make it easier for hackers to figure out how to strip it). Of course, it's been stripped anyway, so that might not be it…

I wouldn't worry too much about it at this point – most people don't even know that Amazon has ANY without drm so they go to other sites to get the drm-free ones.

And someone else said:

If I actually understood DRM, I might be able to comment on it.

Quite. So I left it and didn't worry any more.

2. Confirm Content Rights

Next confirm you own copyright.

3. Upload and Preview Book

Have your Calibre Mobi file out on your Desktop so that when you hit BROWSE to upload your book you can find it easily. When you've uploaded your document, open the Preview Screen. If you have an old Mac, view your formatted ebook in the online previewer. If you have a more modern Mac or a PC, first click the Download Previewer button, then download the book preview file. This will open on your desktop as a Kindle ebook. If you've done your checks at Calibre stage, one quick click-through to check the transfer has happened should be all that's necessary.

4. Enter suggested retail price

For a 70% royalty prices must be between $2.99 and $9.99. For a 35% royalty prices can be between $0.99 and $200.00.

70% royalties are available for books sold in the US and UK. Royalties on books sold outside these territories are 35%.

Getting your price right is touch and go process. Look at the competition, find out what other books like yours are out there, download the free samples. The business way of setting a price is to start high and go lower if necessary. But starting off at 99cents/77p is more likely to get your book into Amazon charts where its visibility will be increased. Initially the most successful ebook sellers were those who pitched low. J A Konrath sold 30,000 $1.99/ £ 1.40 Kindle ebooks in 11 months. UK Authors Louise Voss and Mark Edwards sold 100,000 of their 49p/79 cent thriller Catch Your Death and landed a six figure, 4 book, deal with Harper Collins on the back of it.

5. Hit publish

Wait a few hours and you're on sale, chill the champagne.
If you haven't got a Kindle or a Kindle reader on your computer or mobile phone yet, download free: PC:
http://www.amazon.com/gp/feature.html/ref=kcp_pc_mkt_ln d?docId=1000426311 Mac:
http://www.amazon.com/gp/kindle/mac/download
Buy a copy of your book and read through carefully. If you're not happy with the spacings, go back to your document, readjust and upload again. You can upload, adjust, change the price etc as often as you like.

Welcome to the author's Amazon sales tick. Open the champagne and watch your sales rise with the bubbles. Try not to get addicted to checking those sales figures.

What are Amazon rankings?
Because of the sale and return system of bookselling, the high cost of gathering data and the speculative nature of the publishing business, a cloud of mystery surrounds the sales figures of traditionally-published books not in the Top 100. For many years Amazon sales rankings have been the only way of knowing if your book is shifting copies or not. Many authors are addicted to checking them, especially when they have a new release. One sale can see your rank leap from over 100,000 to 7,000 or from 7,000 to the coveted triple figures. Even if you know it's only one

sale, it's great for the (always fragile) ego. The highest ranking I've ever got is 31, the lowest 4,000,000 and counting. You'll find your ranking under the **Average Customer Rating** row of stars under #**Amazon Bestsellers Rank.** Now, as an independent author, you can check your actual sales figures and accrued income at any time on your Bookshelf.

US Tax Laws

Authors resident outside the US will have 30% of all royalities earned deducted for US tax. This applies to Kindle and Smashwords sales. See the next chapter for more information on how to avoid this.

Getting Paid

Amazon pays monthly, 2 months in arrears, direct into bank accounts in both the US and UK.

CHAPTER 23

PUBLISHING ON SMASHWORDS, APPLE IBOOKS & MORE + HOW TO FILL OUT US TAX FORMS FOR UK AUTHORS (AND SO MAKE 30% MORE PROFIT!)

One name: Mark Coker.
One site: http://www.smashwords.com
See Chapter 6.

Cover image

For your ebook to be eligible for the premium sites like Apple iBooks you need to upload a JPEG, GIF or PNG image of a minimum size. An image sized at 1600 x 2560 will be accepted by both Smashwords and Amazon. The Maximum file size is 20MB. This is one place where a PNG image, which has high pixels, is useful.

How much will you earn?

To get into iBooks in 50 countries including US, Canada, UK, Brazil and Europe, don't forget to add a (free) Smashwords ISBN once your ebook has received its Premium Status. How much income you get from each Smashwords book sale varies depending on whether the sale comes through from Smashwords' own sales site (85% of cover price), from an affiliate sale (via an e-reader, 70.5%) or from Premium Catalogue sales sites like Apple iBooks (60%) and Barnes & Noble.

For a $2.99 ebook you would earn: $2.21 from each Smashwords sale $1.84 from each affiliate sale

$1.27 from each Premium Catalogue sale.

The payments come through on PayPal. Non-residents of the USA will have 30% tax withheld on each sale.

To stop this tax being deducted (in full for some countries including the UK, Canada and Germany; partially for others) you can claim for US tax exemption by sending Smashwords and Amazon (and CreateSpace if you're publishing paperbacks in the US) each a signed US IRS form W8-BEN.

Get the form here:http://www.irs.gov/uac/Form-W-8,-Certificate-of-Foreign-Status

It used to be massively complicated. There are two types of tax numbers: ITIN for individual and EIN for company. It used to mean a visit to the US Embassy. Then some people began getting EIN numbers over the phone and some individuals used them without any problems. Then Amazon stopped accepting EIN numbers. All the ins and outs and wherefores are not needed now, for, at last, the whole system has settled down. You can now simply insert your UK National Insurance number or your UTR (Tax number) in the space on the form where it asks for your ITIN or EIN number. Send the form to to each US company that's paying you money. I filled out 3: for Smashwords, for CreateSpace and for Amazon Digital.

Send the form to each US company that's paying you money. I filled out 3: for Smashwords, for CreateSpace and for Amazon Digital.

Amazon make this bit easy by linking to a sample PDF of the form which you just carefully copy (any deviations from the instructions and your form will be rejected): https://kdp.amazon.com/self-publishing/help?topicId=A1VDYJ32T5D3U4

CHAPTER 24

HOW TO SELL FROM YOUR OWN WEBSITE + THE ARGUMENTS FOR AND AGAINST

My first website was made with the Mr Site Beginner's Pack http://uk.mrsite.com/, the complete website in a package. You can get an e-commerce website up online very quickly that includes your own .com or .co.uk web address for one year, a secure online shop, a photo gallery and blog for £24.99 (for US prices see below). The price includes a year's registration of your domain name, so you just choose your website name and off you go. Crucially for ebook retailers, the shop includes an automatic download link to PayPal. This means that when you make a sale you don't have to do anything. The ebook is sent instantly to the buyer and the money is automatically credited to your PayPal account. If, in the future, you want to change to another operating system you can take your domain name with you for a one-off transfer fee of £15.00.

You don't have to design anything if you don't want to. You're provided with a wide choice of templates that have check boxes for you to decide whether you want your links on the left or on the right, if you want a pink background or a blue background etc. If you want to get more technical you can, but the basics will get you a website up there very quickly. If you want more space and features you can upgrade to Standard or Pro. The Standard starter kit is £39.99 and Pro, £99.99.

There's a phone helpline for when you go wrong. Don't spend hours trying to figure out if something isn't working, phone them up. Yes it's a premium line but I found the guys really helpful and they dealt with my queries in minutes.

The 2 main glitches I encountered were: **Uploading photographs**: if you don't have the '.jpg' at the end of your photo label the picture won't upload.

The Shop: if you alter anything in the shop it will stop working. It took me a while to really take this on board. I thought if I changed a spelling or a price, if I resized the box by moving it along a little, I'd get away with it. The shop will look like it's all there but it won't function. When you've built your shop don't alter anything and test the links.

FREE WEBHOSTS

There are plenty of free personal publishing platforms like WordPress and Blogger.

WordPress is a fantastic system but be aware that you might get advertisements on your WordPress site for which you have to pay to opt out. These ads don't show on your personal page, you have to use another computer to see which ads they've chosen to run. I've been told by other WordPress users that they haven't had this problem, but I have.

These free platforms don't, of course, have inbuilt shops with instant download digital sales either but you can purchase these systems as add-ons. On my First WordPress site I used http://www.withinweb.com/phpseller/index.php ($55, $85 incl installation) (£34/£53), loaded by an IT professional. It's a sophisticated system with many advantages that's easy to use but it needs a server to sit on and you'll need pro help setting it up. I no longer have this set-up:

THE ARGUMENT AGAINST SELLING FROM YOUR WEBSITE

Back in February 2012 I changed the name of blackbirdebooks to Blackbird Digital Books to reflect the fact that we also now sell POD paperbacks, and, abandoning the system of selling from my website altogether, built a new WordPress website. The way ebooks have developed means that PDF sales, which used to be the main format before Amazon & co came along, are now virtually redundant.

All of our sales are via trusted platforms where the customer feels safe in handing over credit card or PayPal details and that's where most readers go to buy books. They don't search Google for a book, they'll search Amazon. So Google SEO (search engine optimisation – in basic language: trying to get your website on the front page of Google), though desirable, isn't such a crucial part of the mix either. My 'making books discoverable' time is currently all spent on working out how to get more visibility for my books on the Amazon website, which is an art in itself (see Chapter 26). When you have a shop on your website you add the extra dimension of hackability into the mix, your website becomes more vulnerable because there are financial transactions taking place there.

This doesn't mean that you don't need a website. A blog-centred website is the best tool you can have to grow your author profile. The latest corporate sales & marketing trends are all about giving back to the customer, rather than the hard sell, which is good news. I recently went to a very useful sales and marketing talk by Sonja Jefferson, the author of a book called *Valuable Content Marketing* which teaches you how to design your website for optimum customer reach. There's lots of good, free common sense advice on her website: http://www.valuablecontent.co.uk/

To confuse matters there are two WordPress setups. Wordpress.com and Wordpress.org. The basic, free simple setup is Wordpress.com. When I say basic I don't mean in terms of design options, there are thousands of templates, with some excellent ones that are totally free (I used the PILCROW theme). What you can't do is add PLUG-INS which are the many add-ons that have evolved over the years, created by the ever-expanding Wordpress community. I wanted an SEO plug-in to raise my website's profile on Google but never reached the moving over to Wordpress.org stage. Without going into anything too technical here, to have Wordpress.org and all the additional add-on advantages, your site needs a HOST, for which you pay a monthly fee. This isn't much, hosts start at around $15./month.

I love thisTyler Moore Wordpress.org YouTube tutorial which is full of fantastic tips:
How To Make A Wordpress Website – AMAZING!
https://www.youtube.com/watch?v=8Jv47_VIBOQ

OTHER WEBSITE OPTIONS
I heard good things about http://www.jimdo.com/, their free website building option includes SEO and a website store and have now transferred my website from WordPress. I'm really impressed. I am using the Pro version which includes hosting, SEO, store, email and a domain address for £60/$99 per year. There is also a free version which I used first to check I was happy (SO easy to use!) and a business version. An advantage Jimdo has over some of its rivals is that the interfaces automatically work on mobiles as well as computers. So any updates only have to be done once.

SELLING VIA THE CLOUD
Websites hosted on the 'cloud' are a recent development and offer the ultimate in storage safety. You pay the company to get you up and running and then pay a small monthly hosting fee:
http://Cloudkb.co.uk.

SELLING VIA A HOST
Another way of selling instant digital ebook downloads is via an online host. http://www.e-junkie.com/ is tried, tested and popular.

Hosting packages start from a few dollars a month. There's also a good Affiliate management set-up here where sales income goes into a central kitty to be shared fairly between the participants.

Relevant to any website:

If you're selling online make sure you're following all legal requirements:

PayPal: If you have a regular PayPal account and want to start trading, upgrade your account to a merchant's account (free).

Trading address: Trading websites must publish an address and contact name and details.

Trading from home: Your rental/mortgage/house insurance agreements may not cover you for trading. It's unlikely but possible that you could find yourself in a situation where you could lose your home. If in any doubt about putting your address online as a business, rent a business address or a MailBox/PO address from your post office.

Techie note

Don't cut & paste from Word or Open Office to web, all sorts of hidden caches get transferred over. If you are making notes offline for xfer, use your computer's free Notepad (PC) or TextEdit (Mac) app (called Simple Text on earlier Macs). Transfer your text > FORMAT > Make Plain Text. Then highlight plain text and paste onto your web page.

CHAPTER 25

SOME TURNING PRO TIPS FOR THE PROFESSIONAL AUTHOR – THE MISTAKES TO AVOID IF YOU'RE OFFERED A PRINT BOOK DEAL

The first international star author was J A Konrath. From bestselling ebook author he's gone to bestselling AmazonEncore print published author. Karen McQuestion was the first ebook author to have her novel picked up by Hollywood. The first ebook $millionaire was Amanda Hocking. The first indies to get their ebooks at both No's 1 and 2 in the UK Kindle charts are my friends Louise Voss and Mark Edwards. And since then, of course, there's been that book – *Fifty Shades of Grey* – which started out as an ebook and POD paperback.

To accommodate ebooks, new business models for signing up authors are coming into play. Rather than a life of copyright deals, authors are as likely to be signed up to fixed-time contracts.

Fixed-time contracts?

Yup....

Here's a food for thought extract from an article by Richard Nash, The Literary Platform 11 May 2010 :....*from a contract that locks you in till seventy years after you're dead, to a three year contract. Renewable annually thereafter. Which means after three years you can walk. Or stay, but stick it to us for better royalties because there's gonna be a movie. Or stay with us because with all the additional formats and revenue opportunities we're creating above and beyond what any publisher has to offer, you're making more money than ever before.*

You see, most publishers have accepted they're not going to make money publishing your book. They're publishing your book and a bunch of other books like it so they can have exclusive rights over as much intellectual property as possible. Such that if, three or five or nine years down the road, you win the NBA, or the Orange, or there's a movie, or an Oprah pick, your whole backlist starts to sell but they don't have to pay you one single extra red percent in royalties.

That's where their profits come from, from being able to NOT have to renegotiate royalties when your books start selling better than they expected.

Publishing Contracts

There are many stories of authors self-publishing their books and going on to land a book deal. The risen star of independent fiction in 2014 is the *Wool* author Hugh Howie who negotiates mainstream book deals on his own terms, keeping his digital rights:

http://en.wikipedia.org/wiki/Silo_%28series%29

He is 'hybrid author' who both self-publishes and has mainstream deals. As ebooks gradually take their place in the scheme of things, this is going to become much more commonplace. Publishing has always been a huge gamble. Ebooks that already have sales figures, reviews and a visibly growing fan-base will become an attractive way for literary agents and publishers to find, nurture and grow new talent. I'd go further and say they could be the beginning of the end of the slush pile. Most publishers' slush piles are already closed. I think it's possible that, a few years down the line, the literary agents' piles will eventually go the same way. Some literary agents have already turned into publishers.

If you are offered a publishing deal, however much your head is turned, get it thoroughly checked and amended by a professional.

Though you may think you've done all the work of finding a publisher yourself, you still have a lot to gain by getting yourself an agent, for many reasons, but at this stage especially because of the way the traditional publishing contracts system works. Find out which literary agents represent the kind of work you are writing and send them a query email. This isn't like starting over and waiting for the pile of rejections. If you have a publishing deal in the offing, agents who are actively looking for clients will be interested to hear more.

This is how it works. If you have a literary agent, the agency will send the publisher what's called a boilerplate contract. This is a contract that favours the author's rights more than a publisher's contract would. The agent and the publisher will then negotiate over familiar well-trodden clauses. Major areas will include the hugely lucrative language rights and territories section.

Traditionally authors' agents always ALWAYS hold on to world rights on behalf of their clients. Traditions are being thrown out of the window all over the place at the moment, but, if you are in a strong position to negotiate, try, whatever you do, to keep your world rights. One of the big ways publishers and agencies (on behalf of their authors) make money is by selling translation rights. Each 'territory', roughly divided up into languages, is a major new market for your work. It's like dunking your teabag over and over again, making more money from the same product. If your book is a bestseller in your own language, you'll go on getting publishing advances and royalties as your book grows and travels. Deals in especially large markets like the USA and Germany can come with their own publishing advances against sales. There will also be clauses on film deals, whether you are liable for legal costs if you're sued, rights reversion to you if the book goes out of print (a tricky area since the advent of digital, because a publisher could argue that a book will never go out of 'print' if it's always available as an ebook and POD paperback and so keep the rights forever) and much more. The Stroppy Author blog http://stroppyauthor.blogspot.co.uk/ features a fantastic series called How to Read A Publishing Contract. She's broken down a standard type of publisher's contract, section by section, and tells you what to look out for. Though of course laws in every country are different (hers is a UK blog), there's lots of good know-how in there for everybody.

See also

Gavin D J Harper's

http://www.slideshare.net/gavindjharper/publishers-contracts/.

A publisher's contract will have royalty percentages weighted in the publisher's favour in anticipation of the author's side coming to the negotiating table. When an agency presents a publisher with their boilerplate contract the negotiating goes back the other way, with publishers pulling back some of the advantages weighted in the author's favour for themselves.

In March 2013 a fantastic new agent and publisher database service called Agent Hunter was launched in the UK by The Writer's Workshop (http://www.agenthunter.co.uk/).

You can sign in for free and take a preliminary look around. Full access is £12.00 a year with a 7 day free trial. The information is detailed, often showing what agents are currently looking for. Highly recommended.

If you don't have, or want, an agent, the UK alternative is to join The Society of Authors. It costs £95 a year, £68 if you're under 35. If you have been offered a print contract you are eligible to join. You will then have access to their legal team. They will look over your contract and advise on your behalf. If you are in the USA The American Society of Journalists and Authors plays a similar role. The Alliance of Independent Authors has a lawyer on hand for member queries specifically related to the indie author. Membership is $99 a year.

When your print book is published by a recognised print publisher you must then join the PLR (UK) to receive annual payments for library loans. It is your legal right to receive a payment from the government each time your book is taken out on loan. I still get PLR on my modestly published novels that came out in 2003/4; at the other end of the scale, I know one author who goes to the Caribbean every year on her PLR bounty. She is not a household name but library readers love her books and borrow them over and over.

https://www.plr.uk.com/

UK print published authors must also join the ALCS

http://www.alcs.co.uk

to receive annual payments for photocopying rights. PLR and ALCS are the closest thing we have to an annual bonus. It costs nothing to register with the PLR and the ALCS deducts your joining fee and their admin fees from your income so you pay nothing up front for either service.

CHAPTER 26

HOW TO GROW YOUR SALES

As soon as you have a final cover, a final draft ready for proofing, and a blurb, convert your final draft into a .mobi and put your ebook up on Amazon for pre-order. You can do this for up to 90 days before publication date. The more visibility you can get before your book is released the better, and you'll have a link for your pre-release publicity. Most importantly, if your book starts to show in the charts sales may begin to snowball all by themselves. Try and categorise your book into a 'niche' category. Whole books have been written on the navigation of Amazon categories (see below), but, basically, if you've written a romantic comedy, for example, rather than going for one of the huge categories like 'Romance' or 'Contemporary Fiction' (you're allowed two) where you don't stand a chance of being noticed, go for 'Literary Fiction, Humor' which has much less competition. More details on pre-ordering here https://kdp.amazon.com/help?topicId=AGSSZQVFKECO5

Publicising and Marketing your ebook is, of course, crucial.

Take the famous feature film statistic: if it costs $100 million dollars to create a film from pre-production to final edit, a further $50 million dollars should be added for sales and marketing. For your ebook replace 'budget' with 'effort'.

A whole subject for a different book. Do as much as you can, read some good books on the subject. Meantime, don't forget:

Smashwords Book Marketing Guide (Free) by Mark Coker

With 26 simple do-it-yourself marketing tips.

For the uber-professional way to do it, read Guy Kawasaki's Mashable piece How To Launch Any Product Using Social Media , http://mashable.com/2011/03/30/product-launch-social-media/ (Then have a little lie down!).

How they did it:
Read a blow by blow account of independent author Amanda Hocking's incredible ebook journey:
   http://amandahocking.blogspot.co.uk/2010/08/epic-tale-of-how-it-all-happened.html
and Scott Pack's story of how one of his books has reached 100,000 sales
   http://futurebook.net/content/confessions-ebook-publisher

Selling:
The problem with selling and marketing ebooks is that it's an ongoing learning process in which the goalposts are always moving. The explosion of new books on how to sell your ebooks (ie digging deep into the hidden depths of the mighty Amazon juggernaut) are there for a reason. It's actually pretty crucial for you to read about Amazon algorithms, categories, do's and don'ts etc if you to have any chance at all of getting your book noticed by readers.

Make A Killing On Kindle (Without Blogging, Facebook or Twitter) by Michael Alvear is one of the best. I don't agree with all that he says but there are quite a few unique, useful tips in here. I see he's got a new one out How To Sell Fiction On Kindle, which I shall definitely be checking out because this man knows his stuff.

Let's Get Visible by Dave Gaughran is the definitive guide to setting up your stall and selling your book on Amazon. I also found The Kindle Publishing Bible – How To Sell More Kindle Ebooks On Amazon by Tom Corson-Knowles really useful.

Both of these books are generous in spirit, offer unique, original, advice and are very well-written.

Coral Russell's *The DIY Guide to Social Media Marketing and eBook Publishing*, doesn't seem to exist any more, but I am keeping one of the most useful links from it here. How to write a book description by ebook superstar Karen McQuestion: http://mcquestionablemusings.blogspot.co.uk/2011/01/my-method-for-writing-book-description.html

The Indie Journey – Secrets To Writing Success by Scott Nicholson with J A Konrath, Zoe Winters, Guido Henkel and other top US independent authors has lots of advice and tips from writers who've been there and done it most successfully.

Thanks to Susie Kelly for the last two recommendations.

Piotr Kowalczyk's blog at http://www.passwordincorrect.com/ is one of the top indie author blogs and has lots of fantastic tips.

'Marketing is merely a catalyst for sales. Like any true catalyst, catalysts help start the fire but they can't sustain it..' Mark Coker

In a fascinating guest post for the blog

Facebook, Twitter

Set up accounts in your author name. Then make a 'Fan' page on Facebook in your author name (and in your book name) and keep all your book-related information and promotion there. Away from your 'real' friends or you'll drive them mad. Become a fan of people in a similar field, or people/organisations you think might enjoy the subject of your book, and post up your news regularly. Keep blatant promotions to a minimum, concentrate on giving to your followers rather than shouting at them. Follow their news and comment on it. Be friendly and creative with your information and feedback.

On Twitter, the # hashkey (ALT + 3 on Mac) is an extremely important promotion tool. Hashkeys group all Tweets under hashkey headings together. Here's a @blackbirdebooks Tweet about a certain ebook publishing guide:

'This is the best book I've read on eBook publishing to date.' US Az ow.ly/xa65f #publishing #ebook #digital #writetip #writing

The ow.ly is a link to the book's sales page on Amazon, the hashkeys gather any news to do with #ebooks #publishing #digital #writing #writetip together under massive worldwide, Twitterwide, listings. This maximises the chances for a RT, a retweet, which spreads the word further. This tweet recently received 17 Rts. Another hashkey I could have used was #amwriting which gathers the writing community together. But it has received so much abuse over time with people promoting their stuff with it I don't think it's at all effective & a bit too cheeky. What I did do recently was a Tweet to promote a novel called *How To Be A Literary Genius* by Jacqui Lofthouse, a satire on the writing world:

smarturl.it/LitGenius #writing must Tweet #amwriting #notwriting #writersblock #tweeting ow.ly/i/5EWzC

Here's another one to promote my blog. To attract a wider audience I've diversified from writing about writing to writing about and photographing the places I go to in London when I'm not writing:

Hidden London – Strand on the Green http://t.co/0Xx8kIgL #London #LDN #pubs #history #Thames #visitlondon

As with Facebook keep promotion to an absolute minimum. Concentrate on giving. Only shouting amidst the chatter if you get really good news about something will ensure you keep and grow your followers. However don't be afraid to repeat the tweet at different times of day, the likelihood of the same person seeing it twice is low. With HootSuite (free) you can schedule your tweets or put them on AutoSchedule to appear when most followers are online. I tend to schedule tweets in bulk these days, putting out 4 tweets a day over 4 days.

My most successful use of Twitter so far has been the tweeting of press release links, both with hashkey tags and also direct to journalists. All journalists are on Twitter now, if you have news, let them know about it. The key word here is NEWS, if it's just promotion they'll not bother to follow your link. In this instance, tweeting direct isn't a spam issue, it's passing on a press release. If you want to source journalists who work in a specific area or for a specific publication, find one who writes for that publication (use Twitter Search) then look at who they follow.

Cover quotes

Print publishers always pester their authors to make shameless use of their contacts to find successful 'names' who can give a cover quote. After I'd sent preview copies of *Done & Dusted* to my closest friends I got some lovely emails saying how much they'd enjoyed the book. The publicist told me to keep all the comments and put them up on the website. I'd never have thought to do this myself. But, heck, they're readers who really did enjoy reading the book. Those that don't like your book tend to not get in touch and stay shtoom if you meet up. So get your own 'cover' quotes going. They're every bit as genuine as those celebrity quotes and it all helps.

Give Your Blog Readers a Free Preview Period

Before the option to put an ebook up for free and Countdown discount on Amazon KDP Select existed, I put a free copy of *Done & Dusted* up on my blog for a limited period. You can do this by downloading your MS to Scribd (free). Then either embed the code into your blog/website or just provide a link to your book's Scribd page. This brought in some great reviews. Another way of getting your ebook out free to friends and previewers is to generate a free Smashwords viewing code and advertise this on your blog/FB/Twitter. If, like me, you opt to enrol your ebook into Amazon's KDP Select program you must not use more than 10% of your content in total over all websites outside Amazon.

Find Bloggers to Review Your Book

Online magazines and blogs, including some very powerful ones with hundreds and thousands of readers, do book reviews.

At Technorati you can find out the influence and authority of blogs relating directly to the content of your book by putting key words into the search box.

Some bloggers have review pages and ask for books to be sent to them, some may agree to run competitions featuring your ebook as a prize, others will state they're currently 'not accepting' . If there's no 'press' link on the blog, go to the 'contact' link to find out more.

The Indie Book Reviewer List, published by http://www.stepbystepselfpublishing.net/ has worked well for me. The independent book reviewer system in the US is very sophisticated and some of these reviewers have become powerful players in the new publishing order. I used the list to source reviewers for my new novel and landed a fantastic review in the Huffington Post alongside Joyce Carol Oates. A million thanks to Step-by-Step Self-Publishing, reviewer Leslie Wright and her US blog Tic Toc.

E-zine @rticles are also worth mentioning, if your book is non-fiction, consider publishing short extracts. Published extracts from this book have definitely boosted sales.

Tagging and Keywords

'Tagging' your ebook with relevant words/phrases makes it more 'searchable'. Tags on Amazon have been phased out but if you write a blog, don't forget the all-important tag words.

You are allowed to list your book on 2 Amazon categories. Finding the most relevant categories that have the least competition can make an enormous difference to sales. You're looking to get into the niche book charts where your book will receive the all-important visibility to readers. A new fiction title that is Contemporary Romance, for example, will be up against 67,000+ other titles and, for a debut author, is really a wasted category. However, if it can fit into Literary Fiction, Humor (6,142 – note the US spelling) you stand a much better chance of getting noticed, especially in your Countdown sales periods where Literary Fiction is featured on Amazon's front page.

Keywords are really important as well. You're allowed to list 7 of these and are prompted to do so when you put your book up for sale on Kindle and Smashwords. These can be single words or short phrases. If you can make short phrases you'll be up against less competition and will achieve a higher Google page (and Amazon search) visibility. For a comedy about a doctor's life, for example, key in 'medical comedy' rather than just 'comedy' . Do some experimental searches using Amazon's search window to see what people are looking for (watch how Amazon fills out the remainder of the phrase, read Michael Alvear and David Gaughran for all the detail.) and read Karen McQuestion's blog piece about keywords here . Experiment. You can go back and change your key words at any time.

Reaching a Wider Audience

A good press release written in the accepted style can be very useful. Blackbird Digital Books has a Blogger Press Release account which is completely separate from the website. This enables us to send a link to the press release on emails and Tweets. We also snailmail press releases to a few major newspapers and special interest magazines as getting through to the top editors via email is very difficult. This has pulled off, getting us one full page illustrated colour article in a large circulation woman's mag – worth several thousand dollars in advertising costs. Blogger accounts are free and very easy to set up. Here's our press release page:

http://blackbirdpressinfo.blogspot.com/.

Keep advertising Tweets general and make sure they're a small percentage of your overall Tweets. Otherwise you'll look really sad and boring and nobody will follow you. Don't send personal promo Tweets or (worse!) send Dms (direct messages) simply promoting your book to magazine editors – or anybody! This is the Twitter version of spamming. If you have news RELATED to the content of your book, that's a different thing.

With a few years' experience behind me now, I think getting good US blogs to review the book is one of the key tools. My experience was that many UK book reviewers and book sites, especially the commercial fiction ones, are not open to anything not published by a mainstream publisher. The US is much more advanced and friendly. Though as time goes on it becomes harder and harder to get a book reviewed on a top site. The UK will catch up, eventually, and I'm sure there are some enlightened ones out there, but I stopped bothering with them some time ago. Keep on searching the internet for blogs that cover the interest content of your book. Create a polite, generic email and keep on sending the email out. The response won't be great so you'll have to keep on sending. One mention of your book, with a link, on a site that gets thousands, or tens of thousands of followers, will transfer to sales. If you can afford it, look at www.netgalley.com, a one-stop site where bloggers, librarians, reviewers go to look for new titles. It's used by all the mainstream publishers and is on my Wish List.

PR

Done & Dusted was the first of my books to have its own dedicated PR campaign. Professional PR is a whole world unto its own. Publicists talk to other publicists, they have contacts and good ones have inspiring ideas you'd never have thought of in a million years.

If you get a break in one direction they'll take that break and work it, turning one radio interview, for example, into several. You only need one of those radio interviews to get the right person listening to turn a local station into a national station that could turn into a TV magazine interview and off you go again. Like mainstream publishers, media producers have lemming-like instincts. They see you on one show and think, oh they've had them on, so can we. With luck the snowball will keep rolling.

It's taken me four print publications, each a result of years of concentrated hard work, for me to start to understand how this all works. With my 2 novels I followed a famous print *What Happens When You Get Published* type of guide. It suggests that you contact your publisher's publicity department some months before publication to ask about their publicity plan. This was a joke. It was hard enough getting anybody to return my call, let alone discuss my particular novel, just one amongst dozens of books being published at the same time.

Publishers' publicity staff are run off their feet and budgets are tightening all the time. The only books that are going to have serious campaigns behind them are the big hitters with established names on the cover. You can't blame the publishers for wanting to publish celebrity biographies, or ghostwritten novels. It's all a huge gamble. The way corporate PR works is to throw good money after good sales. That's why you see posters of books that are already bestsellers on the sides of buses and in the windows of the big book stores. 1% return on 100,000 sales is much more than 1% of an unknown author's sales, however brilliant the book. Apart from the handful of freak hits that spring up every now and then, 'growing' a new author from the dark roots of obscurity is a long and expensive process.

A good publicist will work hard at getting you and your book in magazines, newspapers, websites and on the radio. Try and find somebody who has genuine enthusiasm for your book. They're not cheap, so I think the only way to do it, unless you're rich, is to offer a percentage of the profits of the book. If they're passionate about the product they might agree. Maybe you can find a keen, bright communications student at your local college who wants work experience. Have a face to face meeting and have everything you've discussed confirmed in writing: fees, timescales, work schedules, expenses. Find out how often you'll get an email update on work in progress. And don't think you're 'handing over' that side of the job. You'll still have to put some major effort in yourself. Keep your publicist informed of exactly what you're doing. If they follow up a lead you've already taken action on without telling them, for example, it could be embarrassing and a mark on their professional reputation.

Someone who doesn't agree with me on spending time and money on press releases and PR is John Locke, author of *How I Sold 1 Million Ebooks in 5 Months*. Unlike mine, his PR experience wasn't a good one. His advice on sales and marketing is unique, original and interesting, though my enthusiasm has paled somewhat since he admitted to paying for Amazon reviews – a piece of 'how I did it' information he didn't include in his book. I have a feeling that PR probably works better in a smaller country like the UK. If you're in the US, probably your best bet is to start off by focussing on a part of the country, a State or a city, that is relevant to the book or to the author.

In December 2012 we began experimenting with online PR services. There are many free ones which aren't worth bothering with. You could find yourself inadvertently linked with thousands of useless BOT sites Google Penguin hates. They could penalise your website for by lowering its credibility and ranking. From Wikipedia: 'Google Penguin is a code name for a Google algorithm update that was first announced on April 24, 2012. The update is aimed at decreasing search engine rankings of websites that violate Google's Webmaster Guidelines by using now declared black-hat SEO techniques, such as keyword stuffing, cloaking, participating in link schemes, deliberate creation of duplicate content, and others' . In other words the old techniques for getting your website noticed, offered by companies offering search engine optimisation packages, could now land you in trouble. By participating in free PR schemes your website could be linked to people you'd rather not be linked to. I was not happy with the first paid-for online PR I tried. Nor the second.

In the summer of 2013 I attended a seminar hosted by media communications experts and field-leaders DW Pub (http://www.dwpub.com/). The audience of Prs engaged with a panel of 3 high profile editors – Genevieve Mullen of Real People magazine; Mango Saul of Handbag.com and Stuart Flatt of Average Joe's. This is what I learnt:

Editors' preferred method of communication: Twitter and email:

• If the subject email text isn't eye-catching enough, your email may well be passed by. If you're responding to a DWPub ResponseSource journalist enquiry keep the response heading the same as theirs. ResponseSource is a well-established kind of back to front press release where the editors state exactly what they're looking for and ask for submissions via DWPub emails. You pay to subscribe to emails in your industry category and you then pitch direct to that editor. It is too expensive for non-corporate budgets but it can produce big results.

• If you direct-Tweet an editor (eg @editor), remember they can see exactly who else you're pitching to as well. My most successful 'campaign' was via Twitter, direct-Tweeting a very 'newsy' online Press Release to journalists which resulted in an interview for author Diana Morgan-Hill with The Times, features in *Metro* and *The Daily Mail,* and two guest spots on *BBC Radio Solent.* At the drinks reception after the Q&A session I asked Stuart Flatt about direct-Tweet pitches & he said rather than the Press Release link try and get the whole pitch in the 140 characters allowed in one Tweet. Which makes sense, clicking a link is a whole extra Ask. If they're interested they can contact you via Twitter anyway.

The UK PR industry's paper PR Week is moving from weekly to monthly. This raised questions about where PR in general was going in the future. Is the press release dead? Someone asked. No, was the answer but certain things help. Images help a LOT. Interactive was mentioned, with more fluidity between the media outlets – viral videos a current buzzword 'everyone has a viral video at the moment' . With videos in the mix the PR basics, eg don't send high res images via email, are therefore becoming more complicated. Use DropBox to send large files or something called WeTransfer, also free, which I have used and is brilliant.

So my gameplan for the future is meticulous prep of visuals + thoughtful, careful targeting + killer PR Tweet-wording without links .

A really valuable resource for finding the Twitter handles of journalists and editors, for seeing what is trending in the media and for all-over finger-on-the-pulsery at any given moment is the international PR and journalists' tool www.muckrack.com. Parts are subscription only but some of it is free, including the newsletter.

Groups

Do Authors Dream Of Electric Books A blog collective of 29 independent authors with 3 guest-post authors a month. Updated daily.

The Alliance Of Independent Authors $99 a year membership offers a variety of benefits including meet-ups (UK and US). Access for consideration by an international rights agent. An active Facebook forum. Reduced entry rates to the London Book Fair where there are many group events, some of which their members can participate in.

Advertising

Google AdWords have become a major tool in commercial advertising. They take some navigating. *Google Adwords That Work* by Jon Smith is a useful well-written guide through that particular maze. With a spend of £25 I received £100 worth of advertising. My experience wasn't good. I certainly won't be using them again.

General consensus seems to be that the best places to advertise are the massive websites where readers gather like Goodreads and Kindle Nation Daily. I tried Goodreads advertising, but soon gave up. The Goodreads Giveaway section gets your book more attention, costing the price of a paperback and the parcelling and postage to the winner.

Tips For Getting Your Book Noticed On Amazon

KDP Select. As well as earning a dollar or so every time your book is lent on Kindle, you have 5 days in every 90 days to offer your book for free, or at a reduced Countdown price for 7 days. If you decide to opt in, you're not allowed to sell your books on any other platform for that 90 day period, including your own websites and blogs. US Amazon Prime members can borrow the title for free at any time.

Read more about KDP Select: http://kdp.amazon.com/self-publishing/KDPSelect/.

KDP Select works better if you already have a host of 4/5 star reviews. Before offering ebooks for free, maximise the exposure by informing all the major free ebook listing sites that your book is going free. Some of these sites have huge audiences of hundreds of thousands of readers (Pixel of Ink) (Ereadernewstoday) but they'll only look at your book if it already has a good reputation via the reviews. The Author Marketing Club has lots of useful hints plus this page: http://authormarketingclub.com/members/submit-your-book/ with links to many free ebook registration pages. Do this several days before your book goes free.

BIG BUT: As rules have changed at Amazon, many of the free ebooks sites are no longer operating.

BIGGER (BETTER) BUT ANYWAY:

I prefer the option called Kindle Countdown. Your book is not offered free but for a reduced price (mostly it's [your chosen] $2.99 down to 99 cents). This operates in the same 3-month registration timeframe. You get 7 days on US Amazon and 7 days on UK Amazon (which must be taken separately). The advantages of taking this option over the free option are:

• Fewer trolls. A proportion of the readers who will download your book for free will have absolutely no interest in it whatsoever, they've just taken it because it's there. This leads to dissatisfied readers and the real possibility of nasty reviews. To see this in action, my latest novel's chances in the US had a major setback after it was featured on one of the major free giveaway sites. I was initially delighted at the thousands of downloads. But a whole raft of bad reviews followed. Nothing I could do about it. Another reviewer noticed and suggested it might be bullying. I looked into it further, did a bit of Googling of some of the 'real names' and it turned out the reviewers all came from the same part of the country and belonged to the same Facebook group. A puritanical reading group who objected to the sex. http://amzn.to/1tD9nB0 Worse!: Amazon decided to pick out quotes from the bad reviews to put at the top of the listing. Even though the good reviews outweigh the bad ones. And complaining to Amazon about this got me nowhere. C'est la vie! And Never Again.

• Royalties. Instead of the usual 35% royalty on a 99c sale, you get a 70% royalty for the duration of the offer.

• Your book goes into Amazon's Countdown offers listings on their front pages. These contain many mainstream-published titles as well as your own.

• You avoid the 'ghetto' of free. As many indies have now moved to the Countdown option this is becoming increasingly obvious just by the state of the covers in the 'free' listings.

• There is a possibility of big sales results. If you succeed in purchasing an ad on an (extremely picky) email listing service called BookBub, your investment will probably produce handsome rewards. (See the next chapter on growing sales through the roof.)

To maximise promotion of your other books, add a sample chapter of one of your other books at the end of each book, a mailing list link (set up at Mailchimp, free), and a request that readers leave a review if they've enjoyed your book. Just like the big publishers, offer arcs (advanced reading copies) before the book is published and ask for reviews on US Amazon.

If you have published several books on Amazon and want to make up your own free promotion, you could make a book 'permafree' to attract readers to your other titles. This can work well if you're writing a series: offer the first one free, hook the reader and they'll buy the rest is the idea. For reasons above, it's not something I'm interested in, but it is all perfectly within the Amazon rules if you wish to try it. Offer one book at a zero price elsewhere, most typically either Smashwords or Kobo or both, and Amazon will probably match it with a zero price tag.

One final tip from the world of print publicity:

Most authors are happy to have extracts from their books published for free in exchange for the publicity generated. This is a straightforward deal where the copyright issue isn't a problem. But if you write an article for a magazine or website, or anywhere else, publicising yourself or your book, make sure you don't give away all your rights. Put FBSR on the invoice or in the agreement email. This stands for First British Serial Rights (in the US and Canada – FNASR First North American Serial Rights). It means that the work you've done wasn't just a 'job' for them. You keep all copyright in the article and are free to sell the exact same article elsewhere. To try and sell the same article in the same territory is bad practice and a waste of time anyway. Nobody's going to want to rePublish a piece that's already been featured. But don't forget you've got your world market territories, in English and other languages. Then there are electronic rights and more to consider. There are several good articles on selling international rights, like this one: http://www.writing-world.com/international/intrights.shtml/. As copyright rules vary, find advice relevant to your own country and absorb what it all means before you start trying to sell any articles.

Updating

Don't be afraid to go back and tweek. Though this book is selling steadily now I changed my title recently to make it more Google-search (and Amazon-search; Ingram book catalogue search) friendly – starting off with the exact words that the book is about rather than the empty 'How to' (It used to be called How To Publish An Ebook On A Budget). I've changed the sub-title numerous times; I've updated the content over 20 times and fiddle with the pricing regularly.

When you have updated on Kindle you can ask Amazon to send you an updated version to your account so that you can Proof it.

CHAPTER 27

HOW TO GROW YOUR SALES THROUGH THE ROOF

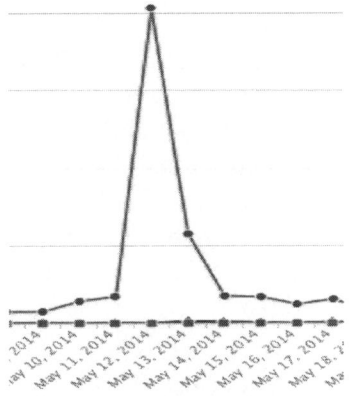

Bookbub/Countdown

The most successful sales method I've come across so far, and I think all other independent authors and publishers will say the same, is to pay for an ad on an e-mail listing site called BookBub. BookBub sends details of your book discount (or free promotion) to its hundreds of thousands of subscribers, filtered by their special declared interests. The ads cost several hundred dollars and they are difficult to get. BookBub are only interested in quality, which is what makes it so successful. Their subscribers know they're getting referrals to really good reads.

Then, as a seller, if you use your Kindle Countdown discount slot to match the BookBub discount day, you will get a 70% royalty on each 99c sale, rather than a 35% royalty which is the norm for a 99c sale. It may sound like a costly inclusion for a book about budget publishing, but, if your book is accepted, you stand every chance of making quite a lot of money. At Blackbird Digital we have had returns of high hundreds and, sometimes, thousands of dollars of royalty income for our most popular author.

The mainstream publishers have cottoned on to BookBub now and it gets increasingly difficult to gain a slot, but they remain open to all-comers and it is well worth pursuing. BookBub doesn't promote new titles, it likes to see a book that has a bit of history – and that means, of course, reviews. So this is very much a LONG TERM strategy.

I have an advanced reader copy list (arc – all publishers do this). I send new titles to everybody on the list and I ask them to post their reviews on US Amazon with the words 'I received this book from the publisher in exchange for a fair and honest review', which makes it all legal in Amazon's eyes. (Friends and family of authors are finding their reviews are being taken down if Amazon discovers a link.) How to build your own list? It's not easy. To kickstart, register your book on the LibraryThing giveaway page. There you can give away 100 ebooks for free (it costs the effort of emailing to each one) in exchange for a review. Not all will oblige of course, in fact only a small percentage will oblige, but the good ones I get seem really pleased to go on the long-term arc list.

BookBub is an American company which operates in the US and the UK with plans to expand to other countries. Keep up to date with the BookBub team at:

www.bookbub.com

and their lively, informative blog at:

http://unbound.bookbub.com/

Selling Rights

The other tried and tested method of making some serious income is to exploit the rights of your title. You could arrange for a translation yourself; you could employ an agent to sell the translation rights to different language territories for you; you could sell your audio rights or you could make your own audiobook.

Translating Yourself

The Spanish language is the second most used language in the United States.

More than 80% of Japan's 94 million internet users have an ebook account at Rakuten (Kobo).

In Chapter 25 I explained why you shouldn't, if at all possible, sign your book away to a publisher for world rights. If they own all rights they can publish your book again and again in each and every language territory.

If you find you have a book that's selling nicely, translation might be an option. Have a look at the world ebook market. Do some market research relating to the content of your book. Translation costs aren't cheap (and don't even begin to think of using Google Translate) but maybe you speak another language, or you know someone who does. The cost of translation means it's only worth doing if your book is already selling very well. Probably the best way would be to find a good translator who likes the book and is willing to translate in exchange for a percentage of the royalites in that territory.

You can sell books from Amazon Digital in French, Italian, Dutch, Portuguese, Spanish, German, Italian, Icelandic, Indonesian and more.

Amazon is expanding all the time. Your English language Kindle edition will now, if rights allow, automatically go up for sale on Amazon.de (Germany) and Amazon.fr (France), Amazon.es (Spain), Amazon.it (Italy) as well as Amazon USA, Canada, Japan, Brazil India, Australia and UK.

There's an interesting discussion at Kindleboards about all of this, see especially Andre Jute's advice half way down the page: http://www.kindleboards.com/index.php/topic,84774.0.html.

Translation Agents

All literary agents have a foreign rights department or work with a specialist foreign rights agency. It's as hard getting a foot in the door here as it is to find a literary agent in the first place. If you were to be successful their department would work with their own network of contacts, selling the rights to your book/s over and over to different territories. There would be an advance for each successful sale; the foreign agent would take a cut and the literary agent would take a cut, but you would still make good money on each sale. (Generally speaking, advances will be in the region of somewhere between $2,000 - $10,000) There's nothing to stop you approaching foreign agents (and, for that matter, publishers) yourself. See John Penberthy's blog piece:

How To Sell $40,000 In Foreign Rights
http://www.bookmarket.com/foreign.htm/.

There's a link to purchase his listing of over 300 agents which I'm sure would be very useful if you want to go down this route. You can also look up any literary agent's website and go to their overseas associate agent pages.

A whole new learning curve. Probably only worth the effort if you've already got good sales figures, or an amazing story relating to the country concerned, to back up your submission.

Online Rights Agencies

These services are a new thing and, unlike the traditional foreign rights specialist agencies, cater for the independent author. The idea is that you list your book/s online and those who are searching to purchase rights will find your listing there and make enquiries.

PubMatch: (Free) I've been registered with PubMatch for a few years now and have never had an enquiry.

IPR License: (£99 +VAT for up to 5 full-length manuscripts + £25 per additional manuscript £10 per upload of supporting materials or updated work. Annual renewal: £60 plus £5 for each additional manuscript beyond the initial five.) In April 2014 I invested some of our BookBub returns by registering Blackbird Digital Books' titles at the company level (£249 + VAT for a year). I then paid an extra £90 for our top-selling title to be featured in their US Book Expo catalogue (this is the American equivalent of The London Book Fair). No sales resulted on any titles over the year and I didn't renew my subscription.

Audio Rights

ACX is an Amazon platform which turns your ebook into an audio book which is then put up for sale on Amazon, Audible and iTunes.

You don't need to pay anything up-front because you can opt for a royalty split on sales with the actor/production company you work with. There are lots of actors there online for you to search through to find the voice you require. If you prefer and have the skills, you can produce the audio yourself. Famous authors like Neil Gaiman and Bob Mayer use this service. They obviously make good returns and I've heard from one author friend that her monthly sales income can be as much as her book sales income. All the info is here:

http://www.acx.com/

I've just finished our first production: Susie Kelly's *Best Foot Forward – A 500-Mile Walk Through Hidden France*. Thanks to Amazon ACX's stipend system, we found a wonderful actress who has appeared in several well-known feature films. If ACX think an audiobook is going to be successful (they'll look at past sales, ranking, reviewer stars) they offer the producer $1000 just to work with you. When this happens you get lots of actors auditioning. Here we have to thank BookBub again for boosting the book sales by thousands. If your book doesn't get a stipend it is, I've heard, adviseable to go hunting for the voice yourself in their audition files and then make the approach direct.

Right, I'm off to preview this book now.

I wish you the very best of luck with yours and hope I've helped.

CHAPTER 28

MARK BINNER'S TOP TECHIE TIPS & TOOLS FOR ADVANCED FORMATTING

In this final chapter, Mark Binner is going to give you a brief 'behind the scenes' tour of advanced ebook formatting. Here you will learn, amongst other things, how to dig deeper into the mysteries of HTML and even how to get an ePub file past the Smashwords formatting police. Over to Mark:

I started learning about ebooks and formatting from an earlier edition of this book. Since then I've downloaded, read and tried out lots of other information on the subject. I will help you to avoid some of the pitfalls that I met along the way. I will tell you about software to make formatting easier, advanced ebook formatting gurus to learn from and great tutorials to help you get to grips with HTML (Hypertext Markup Language) and CSS (Cascading Style Sheets).

Learning about formatting

There is a lot of conflicting information about ebook formatting both online and in books. Also, there are many different models of e-readers available, all with their little quirks. Some people say that formatting an ebook is easy. Formatting a simple text-only book, such as a novel, is RELATIVELY easy, as this book has hopefully shown you, but anything with pictures, hyperlinks, lists, and tables presents a bigger challenge. Previous chapters have taken you through the basics, but if you are not technically inclined, you could use one of the specialist programs to shield you from the complexities of formatting. There are several packages available –which we will discuss shortly – that are reasonably-priced and have glowing testimonials from users.

If you prefer a more 'hands-on' approach, you need to learn a little bit about HTML and its partner-in-crime CSS. If you have already done some web editing, you have a head start. You will need this knowledge to help you to resolve the errors you will see when trying to validate ebooks to make them fit for publication.

In a nutshell, HTML classifies your text and CSS determines what it looks like.

Online learning resources

For learning about HTML, these sites are excellent:

w3schools (HTML tutorial) – the beauty of this site is that is has interactive exercises that show what happens when you change things

http://www.w3schools.com/html/default.asp

HTML Dog (HTML tutorial) – this is another nicely-organised site with lots of detail

http://www.htmldog.com/guides/html/

Both these sites have tutorials for CSS too:

w3schools (CSS tutorial)

http://www.w3schools.com/css/default.asp

HTML Dog (CSS tutorial)

http://www.htmldog.com/guides/css/

Learning from the experts

Here is a list of some well respected authors in the ebook field with links to their words of wisdom:

1.Guido Henkel – you have to read his 9-part series 'Take pride in your eBook formatting'

http://guidohenkel.com/2010/12/take-pride-in-your-ebook-formatting/

2.Joshua Tallent – one of the early professional ebook formatters. See - http://kindleformatting.com/formatting.php

3.Paul Salvette – an American living in Thailand with a rich seam of useful information, especially the bits under the 'Developers' tab. See – BB eBooks http://bbebooksthailand.com/

4.Catherine Ryan Howard – an Irish lady with a great sense of humour and information to match. See – Self-Printing http://catherineryanhoward.com/self-printing-home/

5.Cameron Chapman – Cameron's article on formatting gives some great tips too. Go to http://cameronchapman.com/ebook-formatting-the-easy-way.htm to read them. http://cameronchapman.com/ebook-formatting-the-easy-way.htm

6.Suzanne Fyhrie Parrott – Suzanne's article on 'What makes an eBook formatting expert?' is very interesting. Visit http://www.unrulyguides.com/2012/10/what-makes-a-formatting-expert-formatting-versus-conversion/ to check it out.

Other online resources

YouTube has quite a few video tutorials worth a look, check out David Allen's videos from his site http://digitalbookmaestro.com/

Recommended reading

For Kindle know-how you need to download the two Amazon Kindle books mentioned at the beginning of Chapter 7.

For ePub-based ebooks you need the Smashwords Style Guide mentioned in Chapter 6.

Jon Donahue's free Kindle formatting book on the Jutoh home page http://www.jutoh.com/

The manuals for all the software listed below under 'Commercial software'

Anything free – if you get ONE good tip from any free ebook, it's worth it

Raw Materials

Most computer programmers know that a great way to learn programming is by looking at other people's work and figuring out what they did. With that in mind, here are two places where you can get free ebooks to practise on.

1.Project Gutenberg – thousands of books are available here: http://www.gutenberg.org/
2.Paul Salvette's site BB eBooks has these: http://bbebooksthailand.com/ebooks.html

Tools for creating ebooks

Commercial software

If the idea of learning HTML and CSS makes you want to run for the hills, take a look at the following ebook software packages:

1.Jutoh – this software is available from Antemion Software http://www.jutoh.com/index.htm for £24 ($39 / €30) plus VAT. It can compile ebooks directly in a variety of formats, including ePub and Mobi (Amazon Kindle). There is also an advanced version Jutoh Plus, which is intended for producing ebooks in volume, and has automation built-in. This costs £50 ($80 / €60) plus VAT. You won't need this at the beginning and it can be bought as an upgrade. You can download a trial version to see what you think. Have a look at the support page to find manuals, videos and other useful help. http://www.jutoh.com/support.htm

2.Kindle Writer – the main focus of Kindle Writer

http://www.kindlewriter.co.uk/ is to create an ebook suitable for use on the Kindle platform. There is a 30-trial version available from the home page. It costs £25 ($40 / €30).

3.Ultimate eBook Creator – UEC

http://ultimateebookcreator.com/ takes a similar approach to Jutoh in covering all popular ebook formats, without needing

HTML knowledge. The home page has a 41-minute video with the author talking you through using the software. A 30-day trial version (with some restrictions) is available for download from the main page. The price is $47.

4.**Scrivener** – if you are a writer of any sort, Scrivener http://www.literatureandlatte.com/scrivener.php is surely a must-have tool. Even if you only use it for organising your work, it will help you avoid the 'overload' that comes with trying to keep too much in your head when you ought to be writing. The part most useful for ebooks is the compile function. It takes your document and turns it into an ePub or Kindle, stepping you through the necessary configuration options along the way. It costs a very reasonable £29.08 ($40) for a PC licence, £32.71 ($45) for Mac and there is a Linux version in beta which is currently free. There are also slightly cheaper student licences available too. Documentation is excellent and there are tutorial videos you can download. You can try it out using a generous trial version which covers 30 days of actual use rather than a calendar month.

Free software
Text Editors
A text editor is ideal when using the 'Nuclear Method' (Chapter 6), removing unwanted HTML code or creating your CSS file. My preferred text editor for any purpose is SciTE (Scintilla Text Editor). It's small, neat, fast and uses coloured syntax highlighting to help make reading text /code nice and clear. 'Search and replace' of text is nice and easy using SCiTE too. The project home page is: http://www.scintilla.org/SciTE.html – Windows and Linux users can get it for free but the Mac version is a commercial product costing $41.99.

Other options are: jEdit (Windows, Mac & Linux) http://www.jedit.org/ and Notepad++ (Windows) http://notepad-plus-plus.org/.

HTML Editors

These range from just editors to combined editors and web browsers. Basic editors include Arachnophilia

http://www.arachnoid.com/arachnophilia/index.php

and

Kompozer http://kompozer.net/.

Seamonkey http://www.seamonkey-project.org/ and Amaya

http://www.w3.org/Amaya/Amaya.html are great examples of combined editors and browsers. Visit their websites, read more, download and try whatever you like the look of, and use what works best for you.

eBook Editors

My favourite program for creating and editing ebooks is Sigil. It's free and it has just the right balance between ease-of-use and powerful features. The manual is also very good and there is an online tutorial. Sigil can be downloaded from :

https://code.google.com/p/sigil/

A lesser-known program that has many of the features of both Sigil and Scrivener is Infohesive by 2brightsparks

http://www.2brightsparks.com/infohesive/index.html. It is free even for commercial use but it's a Windows-only program.

My ebook creation workflow is based around Sigil. More of that later.

Miscellaneous software

There are a few other programs that you are likely to need for ebook creation & testing:

1.Amazon's Kindlegen (included as part of Kindle Previewer or as a standalone utility) – this is the only creator of Kindle-format files that Amazon officially supports. It is no coincidence that ALL the commercial programs listed above use Kindlegen to generate Mobi files.

2.Calibre – as mentioned in chapters 6 & 7 – this is a hugely powerful suite of programs that can read, convert, and manage ebooks. It is updated very frequently and the updates often add new features as well as fixes to 'bugs' in the code.

3.Adobe Digital Editions / Kobo Reader / Nook Reader / Kindle for PC / Mac – these free applications are ebook readers that you can use to read and test your ebooks. The first three are for ePub books while the Kindle one is for Amazon's file formats.

More on ebook formats

We looked at the various ebook formats in Chapter 5. I want to add a little about the ePub and Mobi formats. An ePub file is a single compressed archive file (a standard zip file, actually) made up of HTML files, images, CSS files, and various other 'glue' files that act like a sort of master catalogue of what each file does. Due to this structure, an ePub file can be 'unzipped' and edited directly using an ePub editor such as Sigil.

However, the formats used by Amazon's Kindle (Mobi, PRC, KF8) are binary files and cannot be edited directly. Any editing has to be done on the file that the Kindle file was created from and a new binary file created. Knowing this will help you understand my suggested workflow later. Note: software such as the excellent Calibre mentioned in chapter 6 allows you to convert between ebook formats, so you could make an ePub file from the Mobi one and edit the ePub file.

Essentially an ebook is like a mini-website and an ebook reader works like a hardware web browser. In fact, the HTML used in an ebook is a subset of the HTML standard. It is important to be aware of this because ebooks do not support all HTML codes defined in the standard. This could be a trap for an experienced web developer not used to creating ebooks. Amazon has a list of supported HTML and CSS codes in its Kindle Publishing Guidelines. Download the PDF file from:

https://kindlegen.s3.amazonaws.com/AmazonKindlePublishin gGuidelines.pdf

Suggested method for creating ebooks using free software

This method differs from the ones in chapters 6 & 7 because we are creating the ebook ourselves instead of using the automated processes offered by Amazon's Kindle Direct Publishing and the Smashwords Meatgrinder. This allows a greater degree of control (and with that, responsibility) for the author. Both methods have their merits.

First, you need to install some software. Download and save the Sigil installer to a folder on your hard disk. Do the same for your preferred text editor and one of the HTML editors suggested. Finally, download and save the latest version of the Kindle Previewer from Amazon.

** – Use the links given earlier in the chapter (or the 'Links' section at the end of the book) – **. Now, go to the folder where you saved the installer files and install each program on your computer – the order is not important.

Let's assume that your edited and proofread manuscript has been created in a word processor such as Microsoft Word or Open Office. The first job is to convert a copy of that document to HTML or plain text. Saving as HTML will retain the formatting you put in but will include lots of 'bloat' (unnecessary HTML code) created by your word processor that is not needed in the final ebook. Plain text loses both the 'bloat' and the formatting, so you have to add things like bold and italics back in later. Sigil, the ePub editor can work with either file type but not with a word processing document.

If you are unsure which to use, a good rule of thumb is to use plain text for a novel and HTML for a book with pictures, hyperlinks or lots of styling.

1. Save a copy of your manuscript from your word processor as either HTML or plain text. If you saved as HTML, be aware that Microsoft Word creates an HTML file and a folder containing images, if there are any. Open Office / Libre Office create an HTML file and a file for each image (NOT in a folder). After that, you can go to one of these websites to clean up the HTML document you just exported from Word. Take a look at HTML Cleanup Tool http://www.brave.net.au/online-html-cleanup-tool.php/

If you already know HTML well, you can clean up the code directly in a text or HTML editor.

Alternatively, these websites can take a Word document and convert it to 'clean' HTML I.e. remove some of the 'bloat'. They work pretty well but don't handle pictures at all.

Take a look at: Word2CleanHTML http://word2cleanhtml.com/ or Text Fixer http://textfixer.com/html/convert-word-to-html.php.

If you choose this route, you can omit the previous step.

2.Start Sigil and you will notice that there is a file called 'Section0001.xhtml' in the left hand 'Book Browser' pane. If you saved the manuscript as plain text, open it now in your text editor and select the entire document. Copy the selected text, switch back to Sigil and paste it into the middle pane. If you saved your manuscript as HTML, click on the 'File' menu, choose 'Open' and browse to your saved HTML file. Choosing 'Save' from the 'File' menu will result in a new file being created with an extension of '.ePub' . Your HTML or text file will remain unchanged. When you continue to format your ebook, it's the ePub file you will be working on.

3.Using a text editor, create the CSS file that you intend to use to style your ebook. This is where you can decide whether you want headings to be in bold type or centred or in a larger font size. To replicate the look of a printed novel you only need descriptions for chapter headings ('Heading 1' or <h1> tags), and two variations on standard body text ('Paragraph' or <p> tags); one for left-aligned text and one for slightly indented text. Guido Henkel's 9-part guide gives a good start with creating style sheets. Save the file as something like 'mystyle.css' .

N.B. – you don't have to use CSS at all if you don't want to. You can apply styling directly to the HTML elements. This is called inline styling. However, it does mean more work and is not considered good practice.

4.Return to Sigil and right-click the 'Styles' icon in the left hand 'Book Browser' pane. Select 'Add existing files' and browse to the CSS file 'mystyle.css' you created in the previous step. Click 'Open' and the file will be added to the tree below the 'Styles' - you can check by clicking on the little '+' sign. Next, you need to tell Sigil to apply this stylesheet to your HTML file. To do that, right-click on HTML file shown below the 'Text' folder icon and select 'Link Stylesheets' . In the box that pops up, tick the box in the 'Include' column and click'OK' The stylesheet definitions should now be applied to the HTML text.

5.Suppose you have a novel with 20 chapters. The next step is to split the file into separate chapters.To do this in Sigil, position the cursor in front of the letter 'C' in the 'Chapter1' heading and press Ctrl+Enter together OR click on the 'Split at cursor' icon in the top toolbar. Repeat the process for all chapters. Save the file. At this point you can rename all the chapter files from 'Section0001...' etc to 'Chapter0001...' if you wish. Simply click on the first file, hold down the Shift key and click the last file. That should highlight the entire range. Right-click the highlighted range and choose 'Rename' . A box will appear saying 'Rename files starting at..' . Change the contents of the edit box to 'Chapter0001' and press Enter.

6.Now for some HTML. In each of the chapter files you need to identify your chapter headings and mark them as 'Heading 1' - this will be used to create your ebook's table of contents. Open the file 'Chapter0001.xhtml' from the left hand pane. This will display a tab with the same name and open the contents in the middle pane. Select the text 'Chapter 1' (or 'Chapter One' if you used text rather than numbers). With the text highlighted click on the 'h1' icon on the toolbar in the top left corner. The appearance should change immediately. Now press the 'F2' key or click on the 'Code View' icon on the toolbar (N.B. – the icons show a text description when you hover the cursor over them, making them easy to identify). You should see a line that looks like this: <h1>Chapter 1</h1> – this is telling you that Chapter 1 is designated as 'Heading 1' . Press 'F2' again or click on the 'Book View' icon to switch back to the more familiar view. Repeat this process with all the other chapters. At this point all the chapter headings with <h1> tags should have the styling you specified in your CSS file applied.

7.If your paragraph text is to be uniform throughout the entire book, the style you created in step 3 will apply to everything. However, some people like to have the first paragraph of a chapter left-aligned and the rest slightly indented. In a book that has hundreds of paragraphs, most of them indented, the easiest way to accomplish the desired layout is to set the default paragraph style to indent the text and manually amend the paragraphs that are left-aligned. In our hypothetical 20-chapter novel, that would be a mere 20 instances.

8.Now is a good time to add a cover to the ebook. In Sigil, right-click the little 'Images' folder icon in the 'Book Browser' pane. Select 'Add existing files' and browse to the folder where you saved your cover image file. After you click 'Open the image will be added to the tree below 'Images' . Check by clicking on the little '+' sign. Right click the image file and choose 'Add Semantics' then 'Cover Image' . You have now told Sigil that the image is for the cover. You also need an extra HTML file for the cover. To get one click on the 'Tools' menu and choose 'Add Cover' . This creates a file called 'cover.xhtml' under the 'Text' tree in the 'Book Browser' pane. Save your document again.

9.Next we need to enter some basic data about the ebook. The minimum information is book title, author's name and language. If you omit these, the ebook will fail the first stage of the validation. The good news is that it makes a great reminder. Click on the 'Tools' menu and select 'Metadata Editor' . Enter the book title and author name (language should be pre-filled) and press Enter. Save your file.

10.The final step before validation is to create a table of contents (See notes in next section – 'Things to watch out for when creating ebooks'.) If you created one in your Word document and then exported to HTML, it should be listed under the 'Text' tree as a separate file, created when you split the book into chapters in step 5. Rename that file to 'Old-TOC.xhtml' or something memorable. You can use it for guidance when creating a new ToC within Sigil but do not use it in your final ebook. This is to avoid the ToC entries pointing to the wrong place after extra bits have been inserted into your ePub file. Click on the 'Tools' menu and choose 'Table of Contents' then 'Generate Table Of Contents' . You should now be presented with a list of all your chapter headings, each with an 'h1' under the 'Level' column and a tick in the 'Include' box. Each chapter should follow in order; if there are any blank lines untick the 'Include' box for each one or the table of contents will look horrible. Click 'OK' when it looks correct. Click on the 'Tools' menu again and choose 'Table of Contents' then 'Create HTML Table Of Contents' . You will see a new file in the left hand pane. Drag the file to the position where you want it to be in the book structure. Save your file again. Your ebook is almost complete.

11.Validation is done in two stages. The first stage is done within Sigil. Re-open your ePub file if it's not still open and click the big green arrow icon to the right of the toolbar. It should say 'Validate ePub with Flightcrew' when hovering the cursor over it. You can also do this by pressing the 'F7' key or choosing 'Validate ePub with Flightcrew' from the 'Tools' menu. Unless you are incredibly lucky, Flightcrew WILL find something wrong. Sometimes the error messages are helpful and sometimes they are rather cryptic. The error messages do have line numbers of where the errors are, where appropriate. The Sigil manual and online tutorial have examples of typical errors and what to do about them. See section headed 'Common vaidation errors' for further help. When you have eliminated all errors and warnings, a message saying 'No problems found!' . Proceed only when you get to that stage.

12. OK, round two! The next phase of validation is even more rigorous; your ePub file must meet all the criteria laid down by the IDPF (International Digital Publishing Forum). You MUST pass this test for your ebook to make it into the Smashwords Premium catalogue and to be accepted by the Apple iBookstore. Go to http://validator.idpf.org/ and click the 'Browse' button to select your ePub file. Once selected, click the 'Validate' button and wait for the results. If the validator flags any errors, you need to fix them all. If a message appears saying, Results: Congratulations! No problems were found in 'name of your ePub file' ...you have plenty of cause to celebrate. Your ePub file is clean, valid and fit for distribution.

13. If you intend to upload an ePub file to Smashwords too, there are certain rules you have to adhere to. One of them is to insert some Smashwords-specific 'front matter' text at the beginning of your book. Since this is not required in an ePub file for other platforms, like Kobo, at this point you should make a copy of your ePub file. Rename the copy to remind you it's destined for uploading to Smashwords. I'll refer to the original version as your standard ePub file from this point.

14. Open your Smashwords ePub file (from step 13) and add a new blank HTML file after the one called 'cover.xhtml' . Do this by right-clicking on 'cover.xhtml' in the left hand pane and choosing 'Add Blank HTML File' . Rename the file from the default name to 'frontmatter.xhtml' or something similar. Type your front matter text directly into the middle pane and then apply any styling. If your CSS has a style to centre some paragraph text, use that, otherwise inline styling should be fine. Save the ePub file now and repeat steps 11-12 to ensure you have

a valid ePub file. If you were careful you should have no problems. If you do get errors, at least you can be sure they are in the section you just created.

15.The last stage is to create a Kindle Mobi file from the standard ePub file (NOT the Smashwords one). This is very easy, which is why things are in this order.

16.Open the Kindle Previewer program you installed earlier. Click on the 'Open Book' link on the left hand side. Browse to the standard ePub file you created and click 'Open' . The Kindle Previewer will display a message box saying the file is being compiled. It doesn't take long to process. You may get warnings but they are usually nothing to be concerned about. If it fails, however, it usually doesn't say why. If successful, the Mobi version will automatically open in the Kindle Previewer. Remember, besides being a file converter it is a Kindle emulator too.

17.Finally, and most importantly, test, test, test !!

18.Try to look at things from the reader's perspective. Correct even minor formatting errors – you don't want to harm book sales by getting negative reviews. Remember too that errors in the Kindle file cannot be correctly directly. You have to make corrections in the standard ePub file and repeat step 16. For completeness I should mention that you can also convert your Mobi file back to ePub using Calibre but I would not recommend it. Calibre will insert HTML code of its own which will undo a lot of the hard work you did getting it clean.

19.Once you have tested everything thoroughly and are happy with your work, it can be uploaded to your chosen publishing platforms. Well done!

Things to watch out for when creating ebooks
General points
Where standards exist, it would be nice if people followed them. Unfortunately, as so often happens with large companies, people deviate from standards to protect their interests. This is very apparent in the world of electronic publishing. HTML tags that work on one platform may give unpredictable results on others. For example, some devices don't centre text properly even when code has been added to do that. Always expect the unexpected.

I mentioned about cleaning up your HTML when exporting from Word. The same can be said for Calibre. Recent versions can take a Word .docx file (Word 2007-on) and create an ePub or Mobi file from it. It works fine but take a look at the HTML it creates; it's very verbose. Matters get considerably worse if you use different tools too. If some of your ebook comes from Word and some from Calibre, you will have two sources of 'bloat' to contend with. I strongly recommend the 'Keep It Simple' approach and advise you not to mix tools if you can avoid it.

Tables of Contents
There are two types of ToC – the HTML one and the NCX one. There is a subtle but important difference between them. The HTML one is like an index made up of hyperlinks. You can create this yourself or do it in Sigil using the 'Create HTML Table Of Contents' option in the 'Tools' menu. Opinion is divided as to whether it should go at the beginning or at the end – you decide. The NCX version is a navigation map of the book's contents and it's arguably more important than the HTML one. It's the NCX one that the buttons on the ereader device use to move around the book. Your safest option is to include both types. Amazon's guidelines advises putting the HTML version near the front of the book.

Sigil 'bug'

While working on a very tricky ebook with lots of internal links (anchors in HTML-speak) I discovered a problem. Sigil forces you to select some text before it will permit the creation of an anchor. When viewing the ebook using Adobe Digital Editions all the anchors created that way display as underlined as if they are hyperlinks. Clicking on the text does nothing and it looks wrong. The workaround is to switch to 'Code View' and move the closing anchor tag so that it immediately follows the opening tag rather than the selected text. I generated a bug report for this issue with Sigil's developers. You can read the full details here:

bit.ly/17LGc41

CSS text-transform 'bug'

If you use CSS to style your heading text you need to be aware of this too. Say you want your chapter headings with every word starting with a capital letter. You would use the CSS code text-transform: capitalize parameter. However, if the text is already ALL CAPS, this does nothing. To see this more clearly, go to this tutorial link:

http://www.w3schools.com/css/tryit.asp?filename=trycss_text-transform.

Change the line on the left hand side that says

<p class='capitalize'>This is some text.</p> **to say <p class='capitalize'>THIS IS SOME TEXT.</p>**. Click the 'Submit Code' button at the top. Nothing happens. To work around this, use inline styling in Sigil. Highlight the heading text, and choose the icon that is second from the right. Confusingly, the end button's description is 'Capitalize' but the one you need is 'Titlecase' to do what text-transform: capitalize should do.

Kindle-specific points

Features

The newer Kindle models such as the Kindle Fire support over 150 new features via the newer AZW file format. The older models, using the Mobi format, don't. To cater for the broad range of Kindle models your potential customers might own, you have to create ebooks that work on the more basic ones.

Text

1) Unless you explicitly control the level of indentation using CSS, a Kindle ebook will have paragraphs starting with quite a lot of indentation by default.

2) Specifying a particular font is pointless because the Kindle will use its built-in fonts. Also, you need to be wary of the font size limits mentioned in Amazon's publishing guidelines.

3) HTML numbered lists and bulleted lists are not supported on older Kindles. Do them in text, just like the line you are reading now.

Images

1.The different models also have different screen areas which has an impact on how pictures are displayed. Added to that, pictures between certain size ranges can be automatically resized up or down to fill the screen. That may not be what you want.

2.Older Kindles do not centre images correctly but newer ones do.

3.If you want to create an ebook for Kindle you cannot make text wrap around an image at all. You can with an ePub file. Your best option is a compromise which is to centre your images and put text below them. This leads to another problem.

4.Because Kindle users can change the font size of text, you cannot guarantee that a photo caption, for example, will remain on the same 'page' as the photo it refers to. The result can look rather untidy. One solution is to edit the photo with a photo editor and put the caption inside the photo. Then the caption becomes part of an image rather than text. See the end of Chapter 13, the Photos section of this book for details on how to do this.

5.Using images can cost you money. Images take up lots more file space than text. If your ebook has lots of images it makes your ebook file large. If the book is priced so as to qualify for 70% royalties, Amazon will charge you 10 pence (15 cents) per megabyte for your customers to download it. So, a 12MB file priced at £4 would earn you 70% of £2.80 (that's £1.96) rather than 70% of £4 (which is £2.80). Books earning 35% royalties are not subject to this download surcharge.

Validation and testing – things to watch out for

Common validation errors

The Sigil manual has some notes about errors in the 'Validation' section but they are quite general in nature. The following are specific examples to look out for. Usually the affected filename and line number are shown to help you to locate the error. Don't be too discouraged by hundreds of errors because they are invariably the same few issues multiple times.

1.Error message: *The <language> element is missing* and / or :- *The <title> element is missing.*
Cause: You forgot to enter the book title or language in the metadata section. Refer back to step 9 of 'Suggested method for creating ebooks using free software' .

2.Error message: *no declaration found for element 'u' followed by :*

element 'u' is not allowed for content model '(a|br|span|bdo| map|object|img|svg|tt|I|b|big|small|em|strong|dfn|code|q|samp| kbd|var|cite|abbr|acronym|sub|sup|input|select|textarea|label| button|ins|del|script)'

Cause: Your book has a section of text that is underlined but is not a hyperlink. To avoid confusion between the two, this is not allowed. It might seem odd that bold and italic are OK but it does make sense to prevent confusion. Change the underline to be italic, bold or a combination of both.

3.If your book has pictures in and they were inserted in Word any HTML image tags *<img>* might have some invalid parameters inside. Common error messages are:

attribute 'align' is not declared for element 'img' and

attribute 'border' is not declared for element 'img'

You need to remove all instances of *'align=xxx'* and *'border=xxx'* from your ePub file because they are not allowed. Use Sigil's powerful search and replace function to replace all occurrences with nothing (sometimes called a null string).

4.Similarly, you get the message *attribute 'align' is not declared for element 'p'* if a paragraph tag contains *'align=xxx'* . That too has to be deleted.

5.Any of the following messages refer to a font attribute being specified:

no declaration found for element 'font' AND

element 'font' is not allowed for content model '(a|br|span| bdo|map|object|img|svg|tt|I|b|big|small|em|strong|dfn|code|q| samp|kbd|var|cite|abbr|acronym|sub|sup|input|select|textarea| label|button|ins|del|script)'

Also,

attribute 'size' is not declared for element 'font'

attribute 'style' is not declared for element 'font'

attribute 'face'   is not declared for element 'font'
attribute 'color'   is not declared for element 'font'

In each case remove the references to font attributes right through your ePub file. There may be hundreds of instances, so use Sigil's search and replace function.

6. If invalid code exists in the *<body>* section of your ePub file, you might get these messages:

attribute 'link'   is not declared for element 'body'
attribute 'text'   is not declared for element 'body'
attribute 'vlink'   is not declared for element 'body'
they need to be taken out too.

7. Sometimes Sigil objects to certain entries in the *<title>* section right at the start of your HTML file. If you get any errors like the following, remove the entire line in each case:

The <generator> element is not an allowed child of the <metadata> element.

The <created> element is not an allowed child of the <metadata> element.

The <changedby> element is not an allowed child of the <metadata> element.

The <changed> element is not an allowed child of the <metadata> element.

There is one other trap for the unwary – if you use images with spaces in their filenames, your ePub file may pass the Flightcrew validation but fail the more rigorous IDPF ePubCheck test. The safest approach is to use dashes or underscore characters rather than spaces. Most other common validation errors are covered in the Sigil manual tutorials so they will not be covered here.

Testing your ebook formatting

This phase is vitally important and should be done as thoroughly as possible. The quality of the finished product depends on it.

Test Kindle files using various different Kindle models within Kindle Previewer and Kindle for PC / Mac. Set large and small fonts and see what does to the flow of text. Go back and forth to make sure all is well.

Test the standard and Smashwords ePub files using Calibre and any combination of the e-reader programs mentioned in part 3 of the 'Miscellaneous Software' section above.

N.B. – it is **very** important to realise that the software readers are much more forgiving of formatting errors than real hardware e-readers. Something that looks beautiful in Kindle for PC or Adobe Digital Editions may look awful on a real device.

So, test again on as many real Kindle devices (Mobi files) and ePub readers such as Kobo, as you can lay your hands on. Ask your friends to try it on theirs. This cannot be over-stressed. Only when you are satisfied that your ebook looks great on all platforms should you upload it for sale.

Good luck with your e-publishing!

APPENDIX FOR ALAN (83)

THE COMPLETE BEGINNER'S STEP BY STEP ABC OF WORD DOC TO KINDLE EBOOK

August 2011

Dear Ms Zia,

I've just finished reading your book and beginning to wonder if I am not about to bite off more than I can chew if I try going down the e-book route. In your book there is an assumption of computer competence which I do not have.

Maybe I'm mad at eighty three to think of jumping into this pond gripping a life jacket which doesn't fit. Do you know of an A B C book for total beginners? The sort of advice I need is really very fundamental.

Alan

Go Alan! The actual process of going from Word document to finished Kindle ebook isn't difficult. So, assuming no pictures, no funny spacings or anything like that, here's a step by step guide to doing that, pared down to the very basics.

• Get a cover designed. Place an ad in, or look for somebody who knows about ebook covers at
http://www.peopleperhour.com/ (UK)

or http://www.guru.com/

or https://www.elance.com/ (US). Ask for a Kindle cover, and give them this link:

https://kdp.amazon.com/self-publishing/help?
topicId=A2J0TRG6OPX0VM

Ask for a 1600 x 2560 .jpeg

If you might want to make a paperback in the future, ask for a 5.5in x 8.5in 300dpi .jpg – a higher quality image which will cost more.

Don't be afraid to hire somebody outside your own country. Americans are more ebook-savvy than the Brits. Cross-currency payment is simple and safe if you have a PayPal account.

• OK, You have your finished manuscript on Word, proofread, copy edited until it's ready and raw for conversion.

Make A Clean Copy

• First you're going to transfer the document you've been slaving over, correcting, deleting, etc to PLAIN TEXT. This will get rid of any hidden formatting glitches that suddenly make your words appear in places on the page where you don't want them.

MAC: Find the TEXT EDIT Application. Click FINDER (funny blue face at the absolute bottom left of screen). Click the APPLICATIONS folder. Scroll down till you see Text Edit and double click on it. This opens the Application Icon (A piece of paper and a pen) in your control board running across the bottom of the screen. Click on the Icon to open a fresh Text Edit Document.

On very old Macs this App is called Simple Text

PC: On PCs this App is called NOTEPAD.
BEFORE you transfer your text to this document, make a SAFE COPY so that you won't lose all your work.

To make a SAFE COPY :

FILE > SAVE AS > In 'Save As' line write
SAFETYnameofdocument. In WHERE – select somewhere you'll find it easily like 'Desktop' .

Click > SAVE

CLOSE that document.

Now reopen your original final document.

Transfer all your text to TEXT EDIT/NOTEPAD:

OPEN a blank TEXT EDIT/NOTEPAD document

Highlight all your text:

Return to your original Master doc. Click EDIT (right at top of screen) > SELECT ALL

A shadow runs across all of the text.

Now transfer it:

Click APPLE + C (CONTROL + C on PC) which copies the text somewhere deep inside your computer

Move cursor to your blank Text Edit/Notepad page

Click CONTROL/APPLE + V and hey presto it appears on the page.

Your text is now on the page.

Click FORMAT (right at top of screen) > Make Plain Text.

All your fonts and formats will disappear, leaving just the writing.

OPEN A FRESH NEW WORD DOCUMENT don't worry about the page sizes or anything like that, you don't need to bother with that as long as it's a basic, standard kind of a page layout.

Now cut and paste your plain text back onto this fresh Word document.

The text will appear in the standard font you have set in Word. Use a basic, standard font like Times New Roman.

This is now, technically, a clean copy ready to be transferred to HTML. Save it and name it KINDLE-booktitle.

Now, before transferring to Kindle you'll need to:

a) Go through the text and re-insert any text formatting that's been lost like itallics/bold. Don't mess with the spacings yet, leave them completely alone.

b) Justify the margins. Remember, this document will not appear on Kindle as you see it written on the page. The machinery transfers your text in its own way, so only do the basics and you'll be less likely to screw up.

Kindle automatically indents the first line of every paragraph. To keep it simple, therefore, block justify your left margins. In your Toolbar look for the rows of parallel lines, they're called Align Left, Centred, Align Right, Justified.

Highlight all your text EDIT > Select All.

Then Click the first on L icon named Align Left.

c)Now add your front matter, title, copyright etc. You don't need a picture cover inside your document. See Kindle's Simplified Formatting Guide.

d) Now for the spacings. This is where it's a bit weird. Have your text run continuously between each chapter, if a heading within a chapter is at the bottom of the page don't move it to the next page because once it transfers to Kindle the text will keep on running consecutively. Keep sub-headings close together, don't space things out or huge gaps will appear in the kindle doc. What you do need to do is space between the front pages and between the chapters. So when you want a new page click INSERT > Break > Page Break.

e) Check your spacings by hitting the Backward P in your Word toolbar. You will then be able to see where the page breaks are and make sure they're all there.

Don't worry about hyperlinking chapter headings. It's necessary for non-fiction so that readers can jump to the required chapters, but not absolutely necessary for fiction. Don't put page numbers in either, ebook Masters don't need page numbers.

Load to Calibre

Save Word to HTML Web page:

Click FILE > where it says Save As > scroll down to 'Save As Web Page' .

You'll now have 2 files, your Master and your HTML Web Page Master. The latter is the one you load to Calibre. To get your MOBI copy and then load this to Amazon's Digital Text Platform.

So, load your HTML Web Page Master to Calibre, .following the instructions hon page 41.

First, if you have any problems, Amazon digital email help:
kdp-support@amazon.com are helpful and usually quick to respond.

Now go to Amazon's Digital Text Platform https://kdp.amazon.com/self-publishing/signin

If you don't have a reader account with Amazon, create one. SIGN IN

Click GETTING STARTED & FAQs.

Under the GETTING STARTED GUIDE > Publish Your Content

Scroll down to START HERE TO PUBLISH YOUR CONTENT > Enter Your Product Details

And you arrive at the first page of your dashboard.

Bookmark it so that you can find it easily whenever you need to:

Click BOOKMARK at top of screen > Bookmark this Page

1. Enter Details

The dashboard is your control panel where you'll enter:

The title of your book

Click 'Add Contributors' and put your author name in.

Language etc are self-explanatory. Ignore ISBN, you don't need that.

As long as all the work is your own, click 'This is not a public domain work.'

Target Your Book to Customers comes next. Choose two categories that most closely fit your title.

Search keywords: enter up to 7 key words that relate to your book. Separate each one by a comma. Think carefully as keywords can bring readers to your book sales page.

Upload Your Book Cover. Have it ready and waiting on your Desktop – click Browse for image and select the file name.

Enable DRM – click 'Do not enable digital rights management' (see main book for details).

Upload Your Mobi File. Hit Browse and select the Mobi file you made on Calibre which will now be on your Desktop in the 'Calibre' folder. When you get the green tick and 'Upload and conversion successful, click DOWNLOAD PREVIEWER and then PREVIEW BOOK.

A little screen will open with your Kindle book on it.

Now go through the preview window and see how it looks. If you've followed the Calibre instructions you will already have made all your corrections.

Click SAVE AND CONTINUE

Verify Your Publishing Territories

Click Worldwide rights, assuming nobody holds rights in any other country.

Choose Your Royalty. Self-explanatory. For a 70% Royalty charge $2.99 or above. For anything lower you'll need to go for the 35% royalty.

Kindle Book Lending. Tick Allow.

Tick **Accept Terms and conditions.**

Tick **Save And Publish.**

You're on.

It takes a few hours for your book to appear. When it does, buy it and read it through again. If anything's not right, go to your bookmarked dashboard page and upload a corrected version.

You can change your book as often as you like. You can change your price as often as you like. See what other books in your category are charging and take it from there. Good luck!

2 Sept 2011
'I think I've done it and I'm absolutely staggered at how easy it was when I followed your steps and listened to Mark Coker... '
Alan

***** Amazon Review, 8 Sep 2011
Stephanie saved my sanity *I'm 83 years old, technically naive as far as computers are concerned, apart from using Word, and I decided to 'have a go' at getting my book 'The Tree That Walked' on the Amazon Kindle book list. I bought a Kindle reader and half a dozen books which I hoped would help me to do it ... some chance; the first five were totally incomprehensible and it was only when I read Stephanie's words that the clouds began to part. I'd originally allowed myself a week to get up an running on Kindle but, by slavishly following what she advised I was uploaded and accepted on Kindle in a day, with the bonus of being on the Smashwords platform which puts me out into the whole e-book market. Fantastic. I strongly advise anyone wanting to 'Kindle' their writings to buy Stephanie's book. I did and it saved my sanity.* Alan

KEEP UPDATED!
The whole ebook scene moves FAST and this book is regularly updated. I have only dipped my toe into the sales/promotion journey and have, I know, a great deal to learn. I will be sharing what I discover as I go along.

The Kindle version of this book can now be updated automatically every time a new edition is issued. Sign in to Amazon and open any page in the Kindle Store. In the top menu bar, just below where it says 'Your Account' you'll see a Manage Your Kindle tab. Click that and then click 'Manage Your Devices' . There you'll see an 'Automatic Book Update – Learn More' option. Click that and scroll down to 'Automatic Book Update' and switch it on. If you have a Kindle that isn't as ancient as mine, you can also get the book updated there. A tab for clicking will appear next to the book's title whenever an update is issued.

A final word:

The idea for this ebook evolved as I was going through my first, frustrating experience of making an ebook myself. I'm sure that in some places there are better, faster ways of doing things. Hopefully I haven't put in any information or instructions that are impossible to follow. As this book is constantly being updated there may be some formatting errors that seep through. If you have any comments or suggestions for improvement I'd love to hear from you. Please mail me: blackbird.digibooks@gmail.com and I will attend to any corrections that have to be made. Thank you.

Happy publishing!

LINKS

CHAPTER x CHAPTER

Introduction
http://browse.guardian.co.uk/search?
search=Stephanie+Zia&sitesearch-radio=guardian&go-guardian=Search
http://blackbird-digitalbooks.com/
Chapter One
http://www.guardian.co.uk/books/2010/apr/19/penguin-cook-book
http://www.wildproofreading.co.uk/page009.html
http://www.supremeessays.com/prices.html
http://editorsonline.org
Chapter Two
http://www.benedict.com/Info/Law/Duration.aspx
http://www.guardian.co.uk/books/2010/may/01/blake-morrison-lyrics-copyright
http://www.copyrightservice.co.uk/protect/p07_music_copyright
http://www.ascap.com/index.aspx
http://www.ascap.com/index.aspx
http://wikimediafoundation.org/wiki/Terms_of_Use
http://technorati.com/blogs/directory
http://www.huffingtonpost.com
http://www.encyclopedia.com
http://blog.librarylaw.com/librarylaw/2009/07/the-myth-of-the-pre1923-public-domain.html
http://www.webarnes.ca/2009/07/copyright-on-200-year-old-paintings/
http://www.wikipedia.com

Chapter Three

http://www.guardian.co.uk/commentisfree/libertycentral/2010/apr/02/simon-singh-help-me-win-libel-reform

http://www.guardian.co.uk/media/2010/apr/01/simon-singh-libel-victory

http://www.eff.org/issues/bloggers/legal/liability/defamation

http://www.kboards.com/ Writer's Cafe

http://compfight.com/

http://www.freevector.com/.

http://qvectors.net/tag/commercial-use/page/2/.

Chapter Four

http://en.wikipedia.org/wiki/List_of_book_titles_taken_from_literature

http://www.isbn.nielsenbook.co.uk/controller.php?page=123

http://www.nielsen.com

http://en.wikipedia.org/wiki/All_persons_fictitious_disclaimer

http://www.imaginginsurance.co.uk/writers.html

http://www.societyofauthors.org

http://www.authorsguild.org/services/media_liability_insurance.html

Chapter Five

http://www.adobe.com/products/indesign

http://get.adobe.com/reader

http://www.adobe.com/products/digitaleditions/?autoPrompt=true

http://www.futurebook.net/content/lbf11-ePub-3-and-next-big-thing

http://blog.smashwords.com

http://www.smashwords.com/books/view/52

http://www.smashwords.com/books/view/305

http://blog.smashwords.com

http://kindleworld.blogspot.com

http://www.barnesandnoble.com/pubit

http://www.lulu.com/

http://calibre-ebook.com/

http://www.lulu.com

http://www.thebookdesigner.com/2011/01/print-on-demand-createspace-or-lightning-source/
https://www.createspace.com/
http://www.lightningsource.com/
http://www.absolutewrite.com/forums/showthread.php?t=80048
http://guidohenkel.com/2010/12/take-pride-in-your-ebook-formatting/
http://macromates.com/
http://www.jedit.org/
http://www.bookbaby.com/
http://web.sigil.googlecode.com/hg/main_ui.html
http://www.lulu.com/product/paperback/ten-good-reasons-to-lie-about-your-age/16131105
Chapter Six
http://www.smashwords.com/books/view/52
Chapter Seven
https://kdp.amazon.com/self-publishing/help?topicId=A2RYO17TIRUIVI
http://www.amazon.com/gp/feature.html?docId=1000234621
http://www.amazon.com/forum/kindle%20publishing?_encoding=UTF8&cdForum=Fx21HB0U7MPK8XI&cdThread=Tx983EJ889J3B0
http://web.sigil.googlecode.com/hg/main_ui.html
http://calibre-ebook.com/
https://kdp.amazon.com/self-publishing/help?topicId=A1B6GKJ79HC7AN
http://www.dropbox.com/
Chapter Eight
http://www.primopdf.com/index.aspx
http://why.openoffice.org/
Chapter Eleven
http://www.youtube.com/watch?v=Scp5ktP7j34
http://www.instantebookpublishing.com
Chapter Thirteen
http://news.bbc.co.uk/1/hi/technology/8615052.stm
http://www.fookes.com/ezthumbs

http://www.makeathumbnail.com
http://www.gimp.org
http://www.pixlr.com
http://www.picnik.com/app
http://www.rideau-info.com/photos/printshop.html
http://layersmagazine.com/photoshop-resizing-images.html
Chapter Fourteen
  http://pheeena.carbonmade.com
  http://www.bookcovers-design.com
https://damonza.com/
http://www.picnik.com/home
http://www.thecovercollection.com/premade-ebook-kindle-covers/prices/
Chapter Fifteen
http://www.amazon.com/Kindle-Books/b/ref=sv_kinc_1?ie=UTF8&node=1286228011
http://www.shutterstock.com
http://www.istockphoto.com/index.php
http://www.dreamstime.com
http://www.etsy.com
http://www.saatchi-gallery.co.uk/saatchi_online_index.htm
http://www.etsy.com/shop/customgraphics
Chapter Sixteen
http://www.fookes.com/ezthumbs
http://www.makeathumbnail.com
Chapter Eighteen
http://www.thewritingcoach.co.uk
http://www.uea.ac.uk/creativewriting
http://www.deanyjudd.com/literary_chicks.asp
http://www.kate-harrison.com
Chapter Twenty
http://editorsonline.org
http://www.bbc.co.uk/skillswise/words/writing/proofreading/factsheet.shtml
Chapter Twenty-one
http://www.youtube.com/watch?v=Scp5ktP7j34

Chapter Twenty-two

https://kdp.amazon.com/self-publishing/signin

https://kdp.amazon.com/self-publishing/help?
topicId=A2RYO17TIRUIVI

http://macitbetter.com/

http://www.kindleboards.com/index.php?topic=21059.0

http://jakonrath.blogspot.com/2010/03/ja-konrath-kindle-sales-
30k-ebooks-in.html

http://www.amazon.com/gp/feature.html/ref=kcp_pc_mkt_lnd?
docId=1000426311

http://www.amazon.com/gp/kindle/mac/download

http://www.amazon.com/gp/feature.html?docId=1000234621

http://kompozer.net/

http://www.charlescooke.me.uk/web/kz-ug-home.htm

Chapter Twenty-three

http://www.smashwords.com

http://www.irs.gov

http://kareninglis.wordpress.com/tax/

http://catherineryanhoward.com/2012/02/24/non-us-self-
publisher-tax-issues-dont-need-to-be-taxing/

Chapter Twenty-four

http://www.lemoulindelimayrac.com

http://www.mrsite.us

http://www.valuablecontent.co.uk/

http://www.businesslink.gov.uk/bdotg/action/layer?
r.s=m&r.l1=1073861197&r.lc=en&r.l3=1076141950&r.l2=10754
25686&topicId=1076141950&r.I=1076142107&r.t=RESOURCE
S

http://www.withinweb.com/phpeseller/

http://www.e-junkie.com/

Chapter Twenty-five

http://jakonrath.blogspot.com/

http://www.amazon.com/gp/feature.html?docId=1000373401

http://www.karenmcquestion.com/

http://www.dailymail.co.uk/news/article-1362028/Amanda-
Hocking-ebooks-How-unknown-indie-authoress-millions.html

http://indieiq.com/
http://www.theliteraryplatform.com/2010/05/richard-nash-on-a-new-business-model-for-publishing
http://stroppyauthor.blogspot.com
http://www.slideshare.net/gavindjharper/publishers-contracts
http://www.societyofauthors.org
http://www.asja.org
http://www.plr.uk.com
http://www.plrinternational.com
http://www.alcs.co.uk

Chapter Twenty-six

http://www.smashwords.com/books/view/305
http://www.scribd.com/explore
http://nodamnblog.wordpress.com/2010/03/03/so-excited-so-happy/#comment-4512
http://technorati.com
http://www.xmarks.com/about/features
http://www.writing-world.com/international/intrights.shtml
http://www.stepbystepselfpublishing.net/book-reviewer-list.html
http://www.huffingtonpost.com/2011/03/14/book-review-roundup_n_835458.html
http://wrighton-time.blogspot.com/search/label/fiction
http://ezinearticles.com/
http://fessingauthor.blogspot.com/

Chapter Twenty-seven

http://www.amazon.co.uk/How-Publish-Ebook-Budget-Professional/dp/B003UNLBHA/ref=sr_1_1?ie=UTF8&m=A3TVV12T0I6NSM&s=digital-text&qid=1282065472&sr=1-1
http://www.amazon.com/How-Publish-Ebook-Budget-ebook/dp/B003UNLBHA/ref=ntt_at_ep_dpt_1
Www.bookbub.com
http://unbound.bookbub.com/
http://www.kindleboards.com/index.php/topic,84774.0.html.
http://www.bookmarket.com/foreign.htm/.

Chapter Twenty-eight

http://textfixer.com/html/convert-word-to-html.php
http://word2cleanhtml.com/
http://www.brave.net.au/online-html-cleanup-tool.php
http://textism.com/wordcleaner/
http://www.2brightsparks.com/infohesive/index.html
http://www.w3.org/Amaya/Amaya.html
http://www.seamonkey-project.org/
http://kompozer.net/
http://www.arachnoid.com/arachnophilia/index.php
http://notepad-plus-plus.org/
http://www.jedit.org/
http://www.literatureandlatte.com/scrivener.php
http://www.kindlewriter.co.uk/
http://www.jutoh.com/support.htm
http://www.jutoh.com/index.htm
http://www.jutoh.com/
http://www.unrulyguides.com/2012/10/what-makes-a-formatting-expert-formatting-versus-conversion/
http://cameronchapman.com/ebook-formatting-the-easy-way.htm
http://www.w3schools.com/html/default.asp
http://digitalbookmaestro.com/
http://www.unrulyguides.com/2012/10/what-makes-a-formatting-expert-formatting-versus-conversion/
http://catherineryanhoward.com/self-printing-home/
http://bbebooksthailand.com/
http://kindleformatting.com/formatting.php
http://guidohenkel.com/2010/12/take-pride-in-your-ebook-formatting/
http://www.htmldog.com/guides/css/
http://www.w3schools.com/css/default.asp
http://www.htmldog.com/guides/html/
http://www.w3schools.com/html/default.asp
Appendix
http://www.elance.com/?
rid=1R0LP&utm_source=google&utm_medium=cpc&utm_camp

aign=Elance+Brand&utm_term=elance&ad=7529364858&gclid
=CKK4xaf0taoCFRJc4QodMW7A5g
http://www.guru.com/
http://www.peopleperhour.com/?
gclid=COva4P_ztaoCFQoe4QodwXJH6Q

Acknowledgements

Thanks to Sarah Tomley for sharing her editing/proofreading expertise, Jennifer Copley-May for the fabulous Blackbird Digital Books artwork, and to Mark Binner for his valuable additional chapter. Last, but by no means least, huge thanks to Emma Boden for her dynamic energy, brilliant vision and unstinting support.

If you've enjoyed this book and found it useful, please would you consider leaving a review? A couple of lines is plenty. It really makes all the difference to us small independent publishers who rely on word of mouth to get our books known. Thank you!
Amazon USA: amzn.to/11lhgS0
Amazon UK: amzn.to/ZANpGw

About The Author

Stephanie Zia is a writer and journalist who originally trained and worked as a researcher and documentary producer for the BBC. Author of several novels and non-fiction books, she has written for a variety of publications including *The Sunday Times, Which?* and *Woman's Own*. For many years she was a regular contributor to *The Guardian* newspaper's popular *Space Solves* column. Stephanie also runs Blackbird Digital Books, an ebook and POD publisher of quality fiction and non-fiction. Her latest novel is *The Widow's To Do List* about a 50 year old widow back on the dating scene.

Also by Stephanie Zia

Fiction:
Keeping Mum (Piatkus 2004)
The Singleton Mum (*Baby on Board,* Piatkus2003/Blackbird 2012)
The Widow's To Do List (Blackbird 2011)

Non-Fiction:
Done & Dusted – The Organic Home on a Budget (Blackbird Digital Books 2010)
The Easy No-Nonsense Guide to Stain Removal (Make it and Mend it 2009)
Stain Removal: Your Really Useful Guide to Getting Rid of Stains (Hamlyn 2005)
Baby Names Inspiring Names for Every Day of the Year (Hamlyn 2005)
The Decontamination Bible (Sweet Fennel, Taiwan, 2006)

More Blackbird Digital Books

The Valley of Heaven and Hell, Cycling In The Shadow of Marie Antoinette (2011) by Susie Kelly
Best Foot Forward – A 500-Mile Walk Through Hidden France (Bantam 2003, Blackbird Digital Books 2011) by Susie Kelly
Travels With Tinkerbelle, 6,000 Miles Around France In A Mechanical Wreck by Susie Kelly (2012)
Swallows & Robins (2012) by Susie Kelly
I Wish I Could Say I Was Sorry... (2013) by Susie Kelly
The Dream Theatre (2011) by Sarah Ball
Cats Through History – An Illustrated A-Z (2013) by Christina Hamilton
A London *Steal* (2013) by Elle Ford
Schizophrenia – Who Cares? – A Father's Story (2013) by Tim Salmon
*That Special Someone (*2014) by Tanya Bullock
The Modigliani Girl (2015) by Jacqui Lofthouse
The Road To Donetsk (2015) by Diane Chandler
Love & Justice (2015) by Diana Morgan-Hill

Blackbird Digital Books
http://blackbird-books.com/
blackbird.digibooks@gmail.com
@blackbirdebooks

Printed in Great Britain
by Amazon